UTAH POLITICS

PRINCIPLES, THEORIES AND RULES OF THE GAME

JON COX

To my wife Ellie and our three girls, Epuri, Coco and Eva.

CONTENTS

PRINCIPLES, THEORIES AND RULES

Chapter 1 – Running for Office

Chapter 2 – Election Strategy

Chapter 6 – The Church of Jesus Christ Latter-day Saints

Chapter 7 – Consultants

INTRODUCTION

Utah is a peculiar place, and Utahns are a peculiar people.

Men overwhelming dominate Utah business and politics. But it was also the first state in the nation where women cast a vote and is home to the nation's first female state senator (who had to defeat her husband in order to get there).

Utahns drink less alcohol than any other state in the nation, thanks in no small part to the state's predominant faith which prohibits its use. And yet, Utah was the deciding state that repealed Prohibition against the public wishes of Heber J. Grant, the president of the Church of Jesus Christ of Latter-day Saints.[1]

Settled by pioneers trying to escape the world and keep to themselves, Utah today has the highest level of foreign language fluency with international trade a key driver of the state's economic development.

Utahns overwhelmingly believe in limited government and reduced public spending. However, from its initial founding, Utah also has a proud history of supporting the arts, through both public and private efforts.[2]

---

[1] This 1933 Utah vote to repeal Prohibition ironically coincided with the 100-year anniversary of the faith's Word of Wisdom.

[2] Utah's first Governor Heber Wells frequently performed in local plays, often as the romantic lead.

For a short period of time, the state even had its own obscure language, thanks to a distinctive series of letters known as the Deseret Alphabet.

Despite Utah's unquestioned uniqueness, national experts frequently forget that the state's politics are quite different from the national norm. Every few years, Utah has a competitive congressional race. And each time, one of the candidates will bring in out-of-state consultants who completely misjudge the Utah political landscape. They usually go too negative or punch too hard. Other times, they hit on the wrong issues altogether.[3]

They bring the same campaign flyers and stock ads that work in other Republican states, and almost without fail they flop here in Utah. Even the legendary comedian Bob Hope was greeted by complete silence at the 1987 Stadium of Fire celebration for jokes that brought crowds to tears across America but couldn't quite land with the locals in Provo.[4]

It turns out that, in Utah, we're different.

When Utah was first established by Latter-day Saint pioneers, its settlers chose a place where they could be completely isolated from the rest of the world.[5] Within that isolation, it makes sense that the political culture could turn out to be, well, a little bit quirky. This book attempts to translate that quirkiness into easy-to-understand terms, a conversational shorthand of sorts. Instead of discussing the pitfalls of lying, it's much

---

[3] The famous Sun Tzu once said in *The Art of War*, "We cannot enter into alliance with neighboring princes until we are acquainted with their designs. We are not fit to lead an army on the march unless we are familiar with the face of the country—its mountains and forests, its pitfalls and precipices, its marshes and swamps. We shall be unable to turn natural advantages to account unless we make use of local guides." National consultants frequently forget the importance of local guides in understanding the state's singular political environment.
[4] In Utah, we're too polite to boo someone unless attending a Utah Jazz game or the Republican state convention.
[5] Technically in Mexico at the time.

easier to just say, "Stop it with the Derek Fishering." We all know what you mean.

To Utah natives looking to get more involved in local politics or non-Utahns trying to understand how such a peculiar people operates, this book is for you.[6] For those who look in the mirror each morning and see the future governor of Utah, or for those desperate to stop someone suffering from White Horse Fever,[7] this book is meant for you. And for young Utahns wondering how they can ever make a difference in a state like Utah, this book is most definitely for you.

As with any book, it is important to not overcorrect. Utahns are a different group of people, but they do have similarities to the national political mainstream. It is also a people that is continually evolving. What may be true today might look quite different in the decades to come.[8]

Finally, as an author, I am not without my own biases. For starters, I am a cheerleader for all things Utah,[9] and sometimes that might show in my writing.[10] I am a Utah Republican, and I cheer for the home team (except for nativist, sexist, homophobic candidates....you know who you are). But despite my Republican affiliation, I try to be fair. My wife is a Democrat, and she usually keeps me from straying too far into John Birch territory. More than once, I have placed a sign on my lawn for a Republican

---

[6] In studies of the American West, historian Jan Shipps came up with the Donut Hole Theory. This theory describes the establishment of the American West as a donut. While there are many similarities in the settlement of territories throughout the American West, the donut hole (Utah) was different. The western stories of rugged individualism are not the same as the communitarian towns mapped out and planned by early church leader Brigham Young.
[7] See White Horse Fever (p. 16).
[8] I am especially excited to see a new wave of female leaders run the state in the years ahead.
[9] My five-year old nephew still doesn't know my name but instead calls me, "Uncle Utah."
[10] This loyalty was forever burned into my heart when as an 8th grade student in Chicago, Illinois, I wore my John Stockton jersey to school during the team's two NBA Finals runs against the hometown Chicago Bulls. Most of the inscriptions in my yearbooks mention the Utah Jazz and a variety of swear words. I consider this to be one of my proudest achievements.

candidate, while my wife does the same for a Democrat. Our neighbors are frequently confused.

A note to readers, if only doing a cursory review you may find seeming contradictions between some of the theories and corollaries. In all things, there is a place of equilibrium. A candidate who overlearns a lesson today will often be punished for it tomorrow. Sir Isaac Newton would remind us that, "For every action, there is an equal and opposite reaction." The same is true with politicians who sometimes never learn the rule that even their greatest strengths can become their downfall.

While I consider it critical to be approachable as both a person and a writer, I also like to take frequent deep dives on obscure subjects in Utah political history. I try to confine many of these tangents to the footnotes where possible, but I hope you pause from time to time and Google some of the names and events described in this book. If anything else, hopefully it will help you think more about the incredible, and at times offbeat, history of our nation's 45th state.[11]

So with a hat tip to the Bear Lake Monster, Delta Rabbits, and everything else in between, thanks for joining me for an exploration of the principles, theories and rules of Utah politics.

---

[11] I am not the only one guilty of believing in Utah exceptionalism. Utah's Southern Paiutes tell the following story explaining their settlement in the Beehive State. "One day following the creation of the world, Ocean Grandmother, carrying a heavy sack, came to where the wolf Tabuts lived. Ocean Grandmother set down her weighty load and instructed Tabuts and his younger brother, Shinangwav, a coyote, to carry the sack eastward, scattering its contents evenly across the earth. Tabuts decided to trust Shinangwav with this important task and sent him off to fulfill Ocean Grandmother's instructions. Curiosity, however, quickly overcame Shinangwav. He cut open the sack, and people fell out unevenly, in bunches all over the earth. Tabuts, seeing the carelessness of his younger brother, angrily intervened, resealing the sack. The only people left inside were the Southern Paiutes; Tabuts carried them to 'the very best place,' at the center of the world, on the north side of the Colorado River, and opened the sack. There they could find plenty of deer, pinon nuts, and agave to eat. The people liked their new home and decided to stay; that is where the Paiutes came from." Paul Reeve, *Making Space on the Western Frontier: Mormons, Miners and Southern Paiutes* (Urbana, IL: University of Illinois Press, 2006), 12.

CHAPTER 1

SO YOU WANT TO RUN FOR OFFICE

THE WEILER RULE

Every first-time candidate experiences self-doubt.

At the conclusion of the 2018 candidate filing period, Utah Senator Todd Weiler posted a series of comments on social media for the newly announced candidates:

"If you just filed to run for office and are wondering if people are making fun of you, the answer is yes. We are. And that's okay. No one is really 'qualified' before they get elected. Some of my in-laws were laughing at me when I filed for the Utah Senate. But guess what? They're not laughing now."

Known in the field of psychology as the imposter syndrome, this feeling of inadequacy is common in those running for public office for the first time.[12] The same is true in other professional circles when, for example, a person won't apply for a new job because they feel unqualified.

What you might not know about the Weiler Rule is that no matter how successful a person may have been prior to running for public office, they all feel the exact same way. And the feeling doesn't immediately go away once you're elected either.

---

[12] This is especially true for groups not as commonly represented in elected positions. Former Utah State Senator Pat Jones has pointed to this issue as one of the key problems in increasing participation of female elected officials.

A common joke told by various members of Congress, including former U.S. Senator Bob Bennett, goes like this. Soon after being elected, you wake up wondering, "How did I get here?" Six months later, after getting to know your fellow members of Congress, the question changes to, "How did they get here?"

The only way to prove that you belong is to win your election. Stop doubting yourself. Everyone does it, but it is seldom productive.

THE HALLELUJAH CHORUS THEORY

Be cautious when others privately encourage you to run for higher office.

Time and time again, former U.S. Representative Wayne Owens chose to run for higher public office.

He left his U.S. House seat in 1974 in a failed run for the U.S. Senate.[13] After losing the 1984 gubernatorial race to Norm Bangerter, he again won a seat in the U.S. House of Representatives in 1986. But he couldn't pass up on the opportunity to run for higher office, leaving his House seat in 1992 to run again (and lose again) in the U.S. Senate race.

When asked why he kept running for the Senate when the safer option would have been to stay in his congressional seat, the self-aware Owens responded, "When I hear those whisperings in my ear, it sounds like the Mormon Tabernacle Choir singing the Hallelujah Chorus!"[14]

It is quite common for friends, lobbyists and others to privately encourage aspiring politicos to consider running for higher office. Equally common is how quickly those same friends disappear when that person actually announces their candidacy.[15]

---

[13] One of the other candidates who actively considered running for the same seat was a former Republican presidential candidate with the last name Romney who had served as governor in another state. In this case, the 66-year old George Romney ultimately chose not to run despite early polls showing him leading the other Republican candidates (one *Salt Lake Tribune* poll showed him leading the eventual winner Jake Garn 53-16 percent).

[14] LaVarr Webb, "Could Hatch finally be unseated in next election?" *Deseret News*, July 10, 2005. Webb is one of Utah's preeminent experts on Utah political history. I am significantly indebted to him for the tremendous insights and institutional memory he has built over so many years. I hope someday soon he writes his own book on the subject.

[15] Beware the political insider who assures you privately that they are behind your candidacy but is hesitant to do anything publicly to support you. Be especially wary of the lobbyist shop that supports two different candidates for the same race. Too many politicos like to hedge their bets without putting any of their own skin in the game. But the moment your election is no longer in doubt, watch as the floodgates open with support from the very same individuals. Bandwagon fans are bad in sports, but in politics they are even worse.

It is important for a prospective candidate to have an honest self-introspection before running for public office. You should never feel so rushed that you don't take the time to stop and consider whether or not this is the course you and your family want to pursue. The decision is incredibly personal, and while encouragement from other well-meaning friends is always appreciated, never forget that it will be you in the trenches and not them.

Sometimes your private life will become very public. Quite often, many people simply won't care about the election. The latter can be especially frustrating to any would-be candidate.

Like Owens, those already in elected office are especially vulnerable to the Hallelujah Chorus. Winning an election can be exhilarating, but it is important to remember that a feeling of invincibility typically precedes one's downfall. Proceed with caution.

THE MIKE LEE COROLLARY

Political opportunity often only comes once.

In 2009, Mike Lee was a relatively unknown private attorney who had previously served as legal counsel to Governor Jon Huntsman. While other prominent Utahns considered challenging the incumbent U.S. Senator, almost no one in the insider class viewed Lee as a significant threat. However, he chose to take a risk, and today he serves as Utah's soon-to-be senior senator.

Most people tend to suffer from loss aversion. The fear of a loss outweighs any gain, even one that is significantly greater than the potential loss. This asymmetric view of losses and gains has prevented many potential leaders from ever choosing to run.[16] Not Mike Lee. His timing could not have been better, with the country reeling from a deep recession. Running two years earlier or later, and the outcome could have been quite different.[17]

Those who avoid risk will never experience the joys of electoral success. That knot you feel in your stomach right now is a sign that you are embarking on an uncertain future. Good for you. No one ever wins without it.

---

[16] When trying to determine the strength of a potential candidate, I rank them on only two categories: (1) will they run, and (2) could they win. Some perennial candidates run in nearly every election cycle with virtually no chance to win. We all easily dismiss them. But even more common is the very compelling candidate who will never take the risk of running for office.
[17] In politics, it is often difficult to judge timing. In retrospect, it always looks so clear, but at the time you will be surrounded by the fog of uncertainty. For the overly cautious, you will likely never take that risk.

THE C.J. MILES COROLLARY

First-time candidates often overestimate their probability of success.

For years, Utah Jazz fans cringed every time C.J. Miles took possession of the ball late in a game. Never lacking in self-confidence, Miles wouldn't hesitate to take the game-winning shot. Of course, he would almost always miss and dejected fans would return home in defeat.

There is a lesson here for potential politicians. Occasionally a candidate needs to be reminded of how long the odds may be in a particular race. Rather than immediately running for governor or U.S. Senate, try a run for your local city council or county commission first.[18]

While self-confidence is needed for any aspiring politician, irrational exuberance can derail those possibilities before they ever begin.[19]

---

[18] If you get elected to a city council spot, don't immediately begin plotting your way to a higher public position. You will make a terrible city council member, and chances are you will struggle to win that next election. Be aggressive when you need to be, but recognize the ebb and flow of political opportunities.

[19] A corollary to this theory is the talented player (or politician) who has amazing statistics but wants nothing to do with the ball in clutch moments of the game. When the big moments arrive, don't be afraid to step forward. It is during such moments that the truly great ones shine.

THE JULY 22 PRINCIPLE

Every good campaign starts with a plan.

This rule gets its name from the date when Mormon pioneers first arrived in the Salt Lake Valley, July 22, 1847.[20] For those accustomed to the state's annual holiday, Pioneer Day,[21] you may be a little confused.[22] Yes, LDS prophet Brigham Young did arrive in the valley on July 24, 1847, but in reality, the first group of Mormon emigrants came two days earlier on July 22, 1847.[23]

In fact, by the time Brigham Young arrived on July 24 to famously state, "This is the right place," the earlier party had already diverted City Creek, plowed land and planted several crops in the hope of harvesting food before the fast-approaching winter.

Latter-day Saints didn't just arrive in the Salt Lake Valley and suddenly decide to settle down. They knew exactly where they were going. The journals of early church leader Heber C. Kimball even describes a room in the Nauvoo Temple dedicated exclusively to maps of the Intermountain West. He mentions in several entries that Brigham Young was reading in this map room from the various journals of early explorers of the Great Basin. When church members set out on their westward migration, they made specific plans on where they were going and how they would get there. When they arrived, they painstakingly planned out communities

---

[20] That first group of pioneers arrived by wagon, as almost all did during the Latter-day Saint migration. According to University of Utah Professor Paul Reeve, only approximately five percent of pioneers traveled west to Utah by handcart. Feel free to use this fact next time you're assigned to organize your congregation's annual trek.

[21] Or Pie and Beer Day, depending on your persuasion.

[22] Maybe Karl Malone was right all along and the parade really was just for him.

[23] Technically the first of the pioneers, advance scouts Orson Pratt and Erastus Snow, arrived a day earlier: July 21, 1847. If this minor distinction makes you question the legitimacy of the July 22 Rule, then we may have finally figured out why you're never invited to game night with your neighbors.

with wide streets and a grid system unique to the state.[24]

The lesson for politicians is similar. A shoot-from-the-hip campaign is seldom successful, especially with the likelihood that your opponent will have meticulously planned their course of action.

One of the most successful planners in the state was former Governor Mike Leavitt who commissioned specific planning documents including his 1,000-day economic plan for the state. When he became U.S. Secretary of Health and Human Services, he developed a document titled, "500 Day Plan with a 5,000 Day Horizon."[25] Before entering public office, former U.S. Senator Bob Bennett made his private fortune by selling day planners.[26]

A specific campaign plan is critical for any candidate in Utah politics. Candidates often enter a race with high hopes, only to fizzle out when the grind of a campaign drags on.

So get out that Franklin Day Planner and remember, to succeed you must always begin with a plan.

---

[24] Unfortunately someone forgot to tell the settlers of Millcreek about the grid system.

[25] Not to be confused with Cleon Skousen's *5,000 Year Leap*.

[26] Here's a random piece of trivia to impress your friends. Before running for the U.S. Senate, Bob Bennett's only foray into Utah politics was a largely unpublicized 1990 run for a non-partisan state school board seat, a race he narrowly lost to U.S. Senator Orrin Hatch's sister.

THE 49TH STREET GALLERIA COROLLARY

They may look good on the outside, but campaigns are always teetering on the brink of disaster.

As a child of the 1980s, I can still remember the commercials for the 49th Street Galleria in Murray.[27] It was Utah's version of Disneyland for kids like me. They seemed to have everything, and the allure of the iconic glass towers right off I-15 made the building seem that much more attractive.

However, behind that shiny exterior the business frequently struggled, undergoing numerous changes in ownership along the way. Finally in 2014, the towers came crashing down as the building made way for a local charter school.

While it is critical that you meticulously plan out your campaign operations, it is equally important for you to remember that campaigns are chaotic and anything but a steady endeavor.[28] The oft-repeated analogy of building a plane while flying it is very appropriate for most political campaigns.

Your opponent may pivot to an issue you didn't expect. The economy may suddenly stumble. It is impossible to plan for the many possibilities that your campaign may encounter. It doesn't matter how good your plan may be, expect your campaign to encounter the unexpected.

---

[27] Also home to Utah legend David Archuleta.
[28] What is not commonplace is serious campaign infighting. If you can't keep your team together, you won't be presenting a unified message to the public.

THE SERAPH YOUNG RULE

Elections are decided by everyday Utahns.

If you visit the House gallery in the Utah State Capitol, you will see prominently displayed above legislators a massive mural of 23-year old Seraph Young as she cast her ballot as the first woman to vote in modern American history.

In 1870, Utah was the second state to grant women the right to vote, two months after Wyoming. However, Utah's first election was held several months before Wyoming, giving the Beehive State the distinction of being the first state in the nation where women cast a ballot.

Interestingly, Utah women had to win suffrage twice. After adopting it in 1870, Congress revoked the right under the controversial Edmunds-Tucker Act. It would be restored again in 1895, as part of the state's constitutional convention, 25 years before the 19th Amendment would be ratified giving women the right to vote nationwide.

While Seraph Young has a famous last name and was a distant relation to church leader Brigham Young, she appears to be an altogether ordinary Utahn. She was a single school teacher who came early to vote because she had work that day. Beyond that, we don't know a lot about her.

Most Utah voters are similarly anonymous. For all the attention paid to political insiders and wealthy donors, on Election Day those people matter very little. It's the everyday Utahns, like Seraph Young, who will decide your political fate.

THE LIBERTY PARK COROLLARY

Most people care more about their child's soccer game than your election.

Utah political insider LaVarr Webb related an experience of Governor Mike Leavitt in 1976 as he ran his father Dixie Leavitt's campaign for governor. With the primary only days away, the younger Leavitt had the following experience:

"On a Saturday afternoon he was driving past Liberty Park. He looked out the window and almost to his surprise he saw people playing Frisbee,[29] jogging, walking dogs and eating at picnic tables. He recalls becoming almost angry: 'Don't these people know there's a crucial election just a few days away? Don't they know how important this is? How can they be out there playing when there's so much at stake and so much to do?' Then, says Leavitt, he realized he was making a very bad mistake. He was 'in the campaign tunnel.' He had lost perspective, lost his feel for what average people were thinking and doing."[30]

No matter how important the election might be to you, most people simply don't care. They're out walking their dog or watching their child's soccer game. Assume otherwise, and you will make numerous errors in judgment.

Go for a hike. Clear your brain for an afternoon. In the heat of the race, you will likely see the world and your campaign far more clearly than before.

---

[29] See the Pluto Platter Rule (p. 146).
[30] LaVarr Webb, "Winning the Political Game: Stay Out of the Tunnel." *Idaho Politics Weekly*, February 1, 2015.

WHITE HORSE FEVER

The most important skill a candidate needs is self-awareness.

There is an apocryphal White Horse Prophecy in Latter-day Saint culture about a desperate time in the country's future where the "Constitution hangs by a thread"[31] and Latter-day Saints rise up to help save the country. While the original prophecy has been officially disavowed, several members of the faith have referenced the same argument over its history. Many Utah politicians have had the passing thought that the White Horse Prophecy possibly referred to them.[32] Very seldom (if ever)[33] would a candidate admit to having the thought.[34]

Any good candidate must have at least some drive, otherwise they won't put in the necessary effort to win an election. Unfortunately, some of the best political minds can be ruined by delusions of grandeur, or White Horse Fever. If the thought ever crosses your mind that perhaps you are the fulfillment of the White Horse Prophecy, it's probably time to take a little break from politics and clear your head.

---

[31] My dad was a student teacher in a high school civics class when he was a Utah State University student. The teacher he assisted that semester had in the front of the classroom a Constitution dangling from a thread.

[32] Not to be confused with Cavalia, a white horse-themed show from several years ago that took over nearly every billboard in the state in 2016.

[33] Journalist McKay Coppins related the story of an unnamed member of Utah's congressional delegation who once privately explained that it could be argued he was the fulfillment of the apocryphal White Horse prophecy.

[34] In 2004, an incumbent legislator lost his reelection after old letters he had written 20 years earlier were anonymously circulated. The letters included references to the candidate being told by his LDS bishop that he would be "an elder who saves the U.S. Constitution." The letters turned off voters, and the candidate ultimately lost the race.

THE GARY CROWTON RULE

Following a legend often leads to unrealistic expectations.

The words "Brigham Young University football" and "LaVell Edwards"[35] are one and the same. The former coach took the team from obscurity to national prominence, winning a national championship along the way. Today, any visitor to campus passes by the massive stadium with the former coach's name emblazoned across the facility.

As with any legend, at some point in time it had to end. Such was the case with Edwards who retired in 2000 after 257 career victories at the university, ranking him as one of the most successful football coaches in the history of the sport.

Replacing such a legend is nearly impossible, but Gary Crowton tried. At first, the Crowton Era seemed to be on par with the LaVell years, with the Cougars winning 12 straight games to start the 2001 season.[36] However, it was all downhill from there with the team struggling for the following three seasons before Crowton was fired.

Contrast that example with the lengthy career Bronco Mendenhall would have at the school, despite his own series of ups and downs (and annoying press conferences).[37] Even Edwards himself went through serious struggles before his legendary run.[38]

---

[35] LaVell's daughter-in-law Becky Edwards served in the Utah House of Representatives for a decade, earning the respect of Republicans and Democrats alike. It is universally agreed that no legislator communicated more effectively with their constituents than Representative Edwards.

[36] Crowton even had a guest cameo on the film, *The R.M.*, during this initial exciting run.

[37] And weird church things like comparing the team's uniforms to the "Title of Liberty."

[38] Before being promoted as BYU's head coach, Edwards had experienced only four winning seasons in his 18 years of coaching high school and college football.

This phenomenon has been referred to by experts as the "contrast miscreation tendency," a concept that describes a bias in human judgment that occurs due to the act of judging something based on a comparison instead of on its own merits.

It is like a real estate agent who purposefully shows an overpriced, unattractive home to a client with the hopes that subsequent properties will be viewed more favorably.[39] Gary Crowton was always compared to LaVell Edwards, while Bronco Mendenhall was only compared to Crowton.

Remember in a campaign, voters are almost always comparing you to the person you will replace. There's a reason why so many sequels flop when compared with the original. Choosing the Bronco Mendenhall model is much more likely to lead to success.

---

[39] I owe this analogy to investing legend Charlie Munger.

THE STEVE YOUNG COROLLARY[40]

Sometimes a person is gifted enough that it doesn't matter who they follow.

Former Utah sports columnist Lee Benson once described Steve Young as someone who "had this habit of taking the stage in the midst of a standing ovation – for the guy who's just left."[41]

First, it was Young taking the reins as BYU's quarterback from the highest-rated passer of all time, Jim McMahon. The expectations were impossibly high for Young, but he simply went out and matched his predecessor's success step for step. By the end of his time in Provo, McMahon and Young were ranked the number one and two passers in the history of college football quarterbacks.

In the National Football League, he experienced the same phenomenon, replacing Joe Montana, a four-time Super Bowl winner and the best passer in the history of professional football. Young went on to surpass his predecessor, becoming at the time the top-rated quarterback in NFL history.

While it may seem impossible to follow a legend, some people are talented enough that it just doesn't matter. In fact, the challenge might even help them perform better than they would have otherwise.

A good example is former Governor Scott Matheson who followed the first three-term governor in Utah state history, Governor Cal Rampton.

---

[40] I promise the next three college sports references in this book will have nothing to do with BYU. I personally blame the former basketball coach who told me I would be letting down nine million members of the church if I didn't attend the school.

[41] Lee Benson. *The Best of Benson: A Twenty-year Anthology of Sports Writing* (Salt Lake City, UT: Shadow Mountain, 1998), 99. Benson has made a career out of interviewing some of Utah's most interesting personalities. So much of Utah's story would have been forgotten had it not been for his incredible work. I highly recommend his books and old columns for those with an interest in the state.

Many a candidate had attempted a run for a third term, but all of them had failed until Rampton.[42] Matheson came into the Governor's Mansion[43] with very little experience, previously serving as legal counsel to Union Pacific before running for the office. And yet, arguably Matheson is the better known of the two in Utah history.

If you're going to follow a legend, stick with the Steve Young Corollary. Be yourself. Play to your own strengths. And always remember that while taking over for a legend can seem like an almost impossible task, some people are talented enough that it doesn't matter.

---

[42] In 1968, Rampton also officially broke the precedent of two-syllable governors losing their bids for reelections. Before Rampton, every one-syllable governor (Wells, Spry, Dern, Blood, Maw, Lee and Clyde) served two terms while multi-syllable governors only served one (Cutler, Bamberger and Mabey). Feel free to impress your friends with this completely worthless piece of trivia. Rampton even reported that in his reelection efforts, "My primary opponent had a last name containing a single syllable. There were actually circulars distributed during the primary campaign telling Democrats that if they wanted to hold the governorship for more than a single term, they should not nominate a candidate with a multi-syllable last name."

[43] The Governor's Mansion (technically the Thomas Kearns Mansion) is located on South Temple between G and H Streets. Governor Gary Herbert likes to joke that he appreciated the foresight of Kearns in constructing the residence between the two streets in the city bearing the future governor's initials. Also in a gratuitous shout out to my hometown, the Kearns Mansion was constructed from oolite limestone quarried in Sanpete County, just outside of Ephraim more than 100 years ago.

THE WILBUR BRAITHWAITE RULE

Winning isn't everything in politics.

If you haven't ever heard the name Wilbur Braithwaite, set this book down and search it on the internet where you will discover countless tributes about one of the finest Utahns ever to live.[44]

It might seem strange to name a principle about finding comfort in defeat after one of the most successful coaches in Utah state history. Coach Braithwaite held the record for most wins by a high school basketball coach (534) for more than two decades. The National High School Hall of Fame coach won a dozen state championships in his 50 years of coaching tennis and basketball.

Yet many of the lessons that Braithwaite often shared were of the anguish of defeat. In his "Twelve Lessons Learned from a Lifetime of Coaching," Braithwaite repeatedly mentioned the uncertainty of competition, applicable in not just sports but also the field of politics:

- Gracefully accept unfortunate events beyond your control.
- Work hard to influence the outcome of important things within your control.
- The most essential thing in coaching, and a coach's great challenge, is to teach players to never give up.
- Today's heartbreaks turn into tomorrow's strengths.

---

[44] Not a day goes by that I don't miss Coach Braithwaite. Ever since I moved away from Sanpete County as a 12-year old boy, Coach Braithwaite would send me letters in the mail with advice and the latest poem he had written. I always thought I was unique, but talking to so many others I realized he did that with everyone. *Deseret News* writer Doug Benson had this to say about Coach Braithwaite, "When I heard of the passing of Wilbur Braithwaite, the kindly, philosopher-poet-coach from tiny Manti, I opened a drawer in my desk and found The Letters. There are dozens of them, all hand-written except for a few of the more recent ones. I kept all of them. Braithwaite probably wrote thousands of letters over the years to coaches, family, friends and members of the media." Doug Robinson, "Wilbur Braithwaite's loss felt by many." *Deseret News*, 14 April 2010.

For every thrilling political victory, there is always someone else with a similar story of heartbreaking defeat. Such a loss can be emotionally debilitating, especially if you felt a sense of purpose – and even mission – in your decision to run.

This leads to Braithwaite's simple advice, "Never confuse an honest effort in a losing cause with failure."

In such a defeat, you will learn who your closest friends are.[45] You will learn things about yourself that you never understood. So don't get down on yourself in trying times. After all, politics has a way of humbling even the very best.[46]

---

[45] See the Mike Mower Principle (p. 119).

[46] Even when you win, politics can be quite humbling. Asking your friends and family for money isn't something many people enjoy doing. And as Utah State Representative Steve Eliason once said, there is nothing more humbling in politics than a honk and wave.

THE KEM GARDNER RULE

You don't need to be an elected official to make a difference in your community.

Kem Gardner is undoubtedly one of the most successful business leaders in Utah history. If you look over his many successes, you would be shocked to learn he had a single disappointment in his remarkable professional career.[47]

And yet the legendary Utah developer, known for his incredible drive and willingness to give back to the community, had his own experience with electoral failure.

In 1984, he was defeated 62-37 percent by Congressman Wayne Owens in the Democratic gubernatorial primary. While Owens had begun the race with a significant lead, Gardner narrowed the gap in polling and many in the state thought he had a chance to win on election night. The disappointment he felt was certainly tremendous.

Soon after his defeat, Gardner and his wife were called to preside over the Boston, Massachusetts mission for the Church of Jesus Christ of Latter-day Saints. Gardner joked about the call, "At that point, the LDS Church felt if I had four years to be governor, I had three years to serve a mission and sent me to Boston as mission president."[48]

Returning to Utah, Gardner has served on or chaired nearly every board of influence in the state. Numerous buildings bear his name due to his philanthropic generosity. And never once did he ever win a political race.

---

[47] Gardner served as the 28-year old chief of staff to U.S. Senator Frank Moss before beginning his business career. The trust Moss placed in such a young man conveys the high regard Gardner was held in from the very beginning.

[48] It was this move to Massachusetts that led to his close relationship with U.S. Senator Mitt Romney. Gardner has always been Romney's go-to political advisor in the state.

Like Kem Gardner, win or lose, running for political office will change your life. It is common for a losing candidate to receive other opportunities to serve in their communities, often soon after their defeat. Don't be surprised to receive a call from your local city council to serve on the planning and zoning commission or the governor's office to sit on your local university's board of trustees. Whether elected or not, you will quickly realize you can still make a difference.

No matter how down you might feel after a defeat, remember the Kem Gardner Rule and get back up on your feet. There are always opportunities to serve.

THE TRACY HALL PRINCIPLE

Most elections are won with perseverance, not pure talent.

Without a doubt the legendary inventor, Tracy Hall, had both pure talent and perseverance. However, it was the latter that ultimately led to his astounding business success.

A chemist by background, Hall created a process for making artificial diamonds while employed at General Electric. The *Los Angeles Times* compared it to turning lead into gold. Many scientists have since argued he should have won the Nobel Prize for such an accomplishment.

But back at General Electric, Hall was only given a $10 savings bond and no public credit for the invention.[49] Disappointed, Hall left for a teaching position at BYU. Unable to use the same process due to government patents, he stumbled along before eventually coming up with a completely new method for creating diamonds.

Not only did Hall figure out a way to create artificial diamonds, he did it twice.

While Hall could have given up after his company had treated him so poorly, he went back to work until he was able to find a new way to succeed. Politicians should take note. Most elections are won thanks to the perseverance of a candidate.

---

[49] Hall's story serves as the basis for the high school lecture in the award-winning television show *Breaking Bad* (Season 2: Episode 6). The teacher, Walter White, relates the story of Hall, "The man who invented the diamond. All right. H. Tracy Hall – write this name down. Dr. Hall invented the first reproducible process for making synthetic diamonds. I mean, this is way back in the '50s. Now today, synthetic diamonds are used in oil drilling, electronics, multi-billion dollar industries. Now at the time, Dr. Hall worked for General Electric and he made them a fortune. I mean, incalculable. You want to know how G.E. rewarded Dr. Hall? A $10 U.S. savings bond."

A good example is former Utah Governor Cal Rampton, Utah's longest serving governor. Before he was elected as governor, Rampton had lost three different races for the state Senate, a run to become party chairman of the Utah Democratic Party and another race to be the Democratic national committeeman from the Beehive State.[50] Two years prior to his victory in the 1964 governor's race, Rampton lost the Democratic primary for the U.S. Senate by an embarrassing 55-percent margin.

His gubernatorial opponent mocked his frequent defeats in campaign advertisements.[51] But always the dogged campaigner, Rampton never gave up and ultimately won the 1964 governor's race, going on to become Utah's first three-term governor.

If you are down and out, don't forget the Tracy Hall Rule and remember that perseverance is king in politics.[52]

---

[50] Rampton credited one nail-biting State Senate loss to a simple mistake. When the final tally came in, he lost by only a handful of votes. "I learned a valuable lesson. I had more relatives than that who hadn't bothered to vote." Bob Bernick Jr., "Utah's longest-serving governor, Calvin Rampton, dead at age 93." *Deseret News*, 17 September 2007.

[51] On one side of the ad was his opponent's name "Ernest H. Dean" with the word "Winner" followed by various elections he had won. On the other side was Cal Rampton and the word "Loser" followed by five of his recent defeats. The closing line of the ad was, "Who Wins Elections? Ernest H. Dean Does!" Dean went on to lose the election 62-38 percent.

[52] In retirement, Hall and his wife became tree farmers in Payson. Anyone who spends time planting trees in Utah knows a thing or two about patience and perseverance.

THE MR. DIRT RULE

Sometimes a candidate will run not to win but to draw attention to a cause.

In the 1988 presidential election, most Utahns were focused on the two presidential heavyweights, Michael Dukakis[53] and George H.W. Bush.[54] But in Utah, a lesser-known candidate was also running for the office.

Robert Anderson of Magna, self-proclaimed as "Mr. Dirt,"[55] attempted to gather enough signatures to get on Utah's ballot as the Pollution Solution[56] Party's presidential candidate. He threatened legal action when he was prohibited from gathering signatures at the Salt Lake City-County Landfill, a place he described as the perfect location to make his case to voters.

While not always accompanied by such a public spectacle, a candidate will frequently run for office knowing that they will lose. In such cases, they may only be seeking the opportunity to draw attention to issues they care about or to prevent their opponent from a coronation.

Recognizing your opponent's true motives is critical in determining your own campaign strategy.

---

[53] A young BYU student, Jason Chaffetz, chaired the Dukakis for President campaign in Utah.

[54] Upon the passing of President George H.W. Bush, U.S. Senator Orrin Hatch shared a poem he had written for the former president and his wife Barbara:

"You are resplendent in years and worth all the tears,

As we worry – and hurry,

Through each eventful day,

In this great land, made greater still

By God's firm hand, and your strong will

That searched for the better way – every day."

[55] In subsequent public events, he also referred to himself as Mr. Peace and Mr. Earth. We are still waiting for candidates Mr. Wind and Mr. Fire.

[56] I am in the minority on this, but I am usually opposed to rhyming campaign slogans (e.g. Bennett for Senate, I'll Gladly Vote for Jim Bradley).

THE MERRILL COOK RULE

Perennial candidates are seldom taken seriously.

Any time a former member of Congress enters a race, people assume they are an immediate contender. Except for Merrill Cook.

Cook has run for office in nearly every election cycle of recent memory. The political office may change, but the one constant is that Cook is running. By all accounts, he has an excellent résumé including both past political and business success. However, voters ignore that background due to the perennial nature of Cook's candidacy.

Similarly, former Utah Governor J. Bracken Lee also ran for nearly every office in the state.[57] Year after year, Lee was on the ballot, albeit for different positions (governor, senator and mayor).[58] But the difference is that mixed in with Lee's many electoral losses, he had several victories sprinkled in. Cook, by comparison, has lost so many in a row that people immediately write him off.[59]

If you want to be taken seriously as a candidate, you need to plot a viable path to victory. As long as the race is relatively close, your future candidacy will continue to be viewed as credible.[60]

---

[57] Lee also made national news for refusing to pay his federal income taxes as Utah's governor. For good measure he also refused to allow the state to celebrate United Nations Day.

[58] In 1950, Lee was featured in *Life* magazine in a profile titled "Politician Without a Future," where he was called a "self-doomed man." Decades later, he would still hold public office as mayor of Salt Lake City. Lee also said, "No honest man would want more than one term as governor," when challenging the incumbent Herbert Maw. Lee would serve two terms and lose running for an unprecedented third term.

[59] Cook ran and lost six times, before winning a seat in Congress in 1996. On the night of the election, he told reporters, "No one should give up after just six tries."

[60] Occasionally local races will be uncontested in the general election in what is affectionately known as having your calling and election made sure.

THE 1972 OLYMPICS COROLLARY

A longshot candidacy can make sense.

When the International Olympic Committee voted against Salt Lake City's bid for the 1972 Winter Olympics, no one was surprised. The longshot bid only received 11 percent of the Olympic Committee's vote, far short of the needed support to pull off the bid.[61]

It would take the city three subsequent bids before they would win the nod for the 2002 Games.

Similarly, political candidates can often benefit from a raised public profile in a political defeat. In fact, some candidates will run for office knowing they will lose but with the hope of building name recognition for a future run.[62] This is especially true in one-party dominant races in the state. A congressional loss today could lead to a mayor's run tomorrow.[63]

Notice the distinction between this and the Merrill Cook Rule. The candidate has enough self-awareness to understand that the deck is stacked against them, but they believe there is enough upside in running that they still enter the race.

---

[61] The initial brochure for the Olympics bragged that, "Park City has 12 lodges with shops, services and entertainment." Things have changed just a bit in the last few years in Utah.

[62] Some candidates will even run for governor in hopes of being selected as a lieutenant governor running mate.

[63] This rule is especially true if you lose to a political legend (pretty much the entire plot of *Rocky I*). Mitt Romney may have lost to Senator Ted Kennedy in Massachusetts, but the close race certainly made Romney a contender in future statewide elections. The most transparent politician I have seen on this front was former gubernatorial candidate Bob Springmeyer who challenged the popular incumbent Governor Jon Huntsman in 2008. In filing for office, the Democrat Springmeyer told the *Deseret News*, "I told the party that I would gladly step down if some good, strong Democrat wanted to win by losing...Someone who wanted to set up a good foundation for running in four years. But that doesn't seem to be happening."

THE SIXTH GENERATION RULE

You don't have to be from Utah to run in Utah.

During the 2014 election to replace outgoing Representative Jim
Matheson, Democratic candidate Doug Owens never left an audience
without reminding them that he was a sixth-generation Utahn. His
campaign website proudly trumpeted the same message, and before the
election was over, Owens would air numerous commercials with the same
"sixth-generation Utahn" line prominently featured.

As the daughter of Haitian immigrants, his Republican opponent, Mia
Love, could not make the same claim. On Election Day, Utah voters
didn't seem to care, sending Love to Congress over Owens. Go through a
list of recent members of Congress in Utah and you will see how frequent
it is for Utahns to elect recent transplants to the state:

- **Senator Mitt Romney** - Massachusetts
- **Senator Orrin Hatch** - Pennsylvania.[64]
- **Senator Mike Lee** - Washington, D.C. and Utah County
- **Representative Mia Love** - New York and Connecticut[65]
- **Representative Rob Bishop** - Davis County
- **Representative Chris Stewart** - Cache County
- **Representative John Curtis** - Salt Lake County
- **Representative Jason Chaffetz** - California[66]

---

[64] While in later years, Hatch never shied away from his Pittsburgh background, his official
biography reminded voters that he was one of them. "Orrin Grant Hatch was born on March
22, 1934 to Jesse and Helen Hatch. His great-grandfather, Jeremiah Hatch, founded what is
now known as Vernal, located in eastern Utah's great Uintah basin. Senator Hatch married the
former Elaine Hansen of Newton, Utah." When repeatedly criticized for it in his 1976 race,
Hatch's mother even went so far as to write a *Deseret News* letter to the editor saying she was to
blame for Hatch not growing up in the state.
[65] In 2018, Love was defeated by Democrat Ben McAdams. The West Bountiful native never
made an issue of his opponent's background.
[66] Chaffetz is from Los Gatos, California. If someone can be elected from a place called The
Cats, California, I clearly know nothing about Utah politics.

Given Utah's occasional reputation for being too insular, this fact can be quite refreshing. Honestly, no one even asks the question if a person is from Utah or not. Of course, in local races, especially in rural Utah, this is not always the case.[67] And our track record with governors has been less diverse, with the overwhelming majority raised in the Beehive State.[68]

But the charge of carpet bagging[69] just doesn't seem to stick in Utah. Don't waste your money on the attack.

---

[67] See the Reverse Dog Year Rule (p. 67).

[68] According to my math, the last governor not born in Utah was Scott Matheson, but he was raised in Utah from a very young age. Before that, you have to go all the way back to George Dern* to find a governor not born and raised in the state. Since he was first elected before the Depression, the "Sixth Generation Rule" might not apply to the governor's race.

[69] If you want to learn how not to give a good convention speech, look no further than the 2018 U.S. Senate race where a candidate dedicated his entire speech to a carpet bagging prop. In general, I would encourage you to avoid props altogether (unless your name is Randy Horiuchi, see p. 55). One candidate for governor in 1992 gave every convention speech dressed in a chain-and-ball prop. That same candidate went on to become a close confidante of Attorney General Mark Shurtleff, going so far as to call himself the Attorney General's "Porter Rockwell."

*In a piece of random George Dern trivia, his great-granddaughter Laura Dern is a famous actress who is perhaps best known as the female lead in the movie *Jurassic Park*. Her father (and grandson of the former governor), Bruce Dern, also enjoyed a long acting career, including such roles as one of the main characters in *The Burbs* and Joe Kennedy in *Chappaquiddick*.

THE EASTONIAN RULE

There is power in proximity.

As you open the 1951 East High School yearbook, *The Eastonian*, and look at the senior class, you will find two different U.S. Senators (Jake Garn and Bob Bennett) and a member of the First Presidency of the Church of Jesus Christ of Latter-day Saints (Henry B. Eyring) on the very same page.[70]

In the same yearbook, you will find other prominent Utahns, including U.S. Congressman Jim Hansen, Chief Justice of the Utah Supreme Court Dan Stewart and Dixie State College University President Doug Alder. One student, Don Gale, who dropped out of the class would later go on to become one of Utah's most prolific writers and the public face of KSL-TV's editorials for decades to come.

It might not be fair but being close to power exponentially increases the likelihood that you too will be powerful. Mike Lee's church home teacher was former Senate Majority Leader Harry Reid.[71] As a young child, Governor Cal Rampton lived next door to Governor Charles Mabey.

Each of these individuals was immensely qualified and worked hard to achieve their extraordinary professional success. However, as the Eastonian Rule demonstrates, it never hurts to be close to power.[72]

---

[70] At the funeral of Senator Bennett, President Eyring related an experience from high school where both he and Bennett performed a skit together, "He was Dean Martin, and I was Jerry Lewis," Eyring said. "But we'll not talk about that."

[71] His father was also a prominent appointee in the Reagan administration, former BYU president and by all accounts one of the most extraordinary legal minds in state history.

[72] Take a look at the 1970 *Eastonian* yearbook if you want to see television celebrity Roseanne Barr as a high school junior.

THE ROY SIMMONS COROLLARY

Some of Utah's most important leaders come from disadvantaged backgrounds.

From a young age, Roy Simmons knew more tragedy than most Utahns will experience in a lifetime. Adopted at birth by a poor blacksmith's helper, his adopted mother died when he was only 8 years old, and his father passed away soon thereafter. Raised by a family friend, Simmons would go on to become one of Utah's most successful business leaders as chairman of the board and CEO of Zions Bank for 42 years.

Those closest to him attribute this unparalleled success to his legendary work ethic.[73] Always the entrepreneur, by the time he entered high school Simmons had held 37 different jobs.

In a speech honoring Simmons, former LDS Church President Harold B. Lee said, "To know Roy Simmons and the story of his humble background and his early life, and to know that by his own ingenuity and his own thrift and industry he has become one of the most respected citizens of this community, is to know the heart of this man."

For those not born into wealth or prosperity, the thought of succeeding in business or politics can seem impossible. But on those days when perhaps you are feeling down and overwhelmed by insurmountable odds, remember the Roy Simmons story. Some of Utah's finest leaders have come from the most improbable of places.[74] You could be next.

---

[73] His obituary said his wife Tibby's only complaint of her husband was his penchant for burning whatever he tried to cook. She joked that his epitaph about both his cooking and life should read, "He always cooked on high heat." His legendary energy and drive has been unmatched in the history of the state's business leaders.

[74] Another improbable Utah success story was the best friend and business partner of Simmons, I.J. "Izzy" Wagner. To learn more about this inspiring man's life, read Don Gale's excellent book, *Bags to Riches: The Story of I.J. Wagner.*

THE GREAT MENTIONERS COROLLARY

The parlor game of politics is heavily influenced by a very small group of people.

Every politician wants their name to be mentioned in the discussion of a future political contest. Whether or not they end up running doesn't matter as much as the fact that people view them as a viable contender. Many politicos have made a career out of this constant mentioning, building relevance without ever taking the plunge of actually running.

A prominent *Deseret News* writer astutely referred to this small group of political prognosticators as the "Great Mentioners." It essentially consists of the same subset of individuals a political writer turns to for a quote about the political issue of the day.[75] Inevitably this gives the insider a significant amount of influence in deciding who gets mentioned and who doesn't.

One of Utah's most respected voices among the "Great Mentioners" was longtime Hinckley Institute of Politics Director Kirk Jowers. The perpetually-friendly Jowers could always be depended on to give reporters a substantive quote on a moment's notice. When a competitive election arrived, those same reporters turned to Jowers for his insights on what candidates to watch for in the race (occasionally including Jowers himself).

Aspiring politicos frequently try to gain favor with the "Great Mentioners" in hopes of being named in the next discussion of an open seat. This outsized influence does not necessarily reflect the views of the broader audience of Utahns, especially in the very early stages of an election.

---

[75] This situation can become somewhat comical when the independent expert asked to comment for the story is actively considering a run for the very same elected office.

THE MATHESON COROLLARY

Early poll numbers in an open race are a poor predictor of the likely winner.

For those who believe political office is only for the rich and famous, Utah political history gives us some examples to show that isn't always the case.

At the beginning of the race to replace outgoing Governor Cal Rampton, Union Pacific attorney Scott Matheson initially received a meager 1.5 percent in a statewide poll of the race. Yet, the eventual successor of Governor Rampton went on to become one of Utah's most popular politicians.[76] The Matheson name now carries considerable political weight, but that wasn't the case when Matheson first ran for public office.

During the 1992 open gubernatorial race, Mike Leavitt started out polling at just one percent. Several months after declaring his candidacy for the open Senate race in 1992, Bob Bennett was polling at a meager three percent of public support. It is important to note that while the public didn't know them, in each of these cases the candidates enjoyed key support from established political figures.

The lesson in politics (especially in an open seat) is to always watch for the dark horse. More often than not, they end up surprising all of us.

---

[76] If I could choose one deceased Utah politician I would like to have met, it would be Matheson. He was an icon who passed away far too early at age 61, the victim of a cancer possibly contracted as a result of downwind exposure to nuclear fallout in his native southern Utah.

THE KANAB CITY COUNCIL PRINCIPLE

Utah women have made history before, and they will again.

In 1911, Kanab, Utah became the first town in America to have an all-female city council and mayor. The council worked hard during their two years together, implementing a wide variety of policies in the small Utah town.[77]

Elected on that historic day was Tamar Hamblin, Luella McAllister, Blanche Hamblin, Vinnie Jepson, and Mary Chamberlain, with Chamberlain serving as mayor. Jepson would soon be replaced by Ada Pratt Seegmiller, who served out the duration of her term.

An article written by prominent Utah historian Paul Reeve[78] reported the following about the council:

"The female board spent an active two years in office, leading some supporters to claim that they had done more for Kanab than all the previous boards combined. Their first official act was to protect local merchants by increasing the license fee for peddlers and traveling salespeople. Other ordinances included the regulation of stray animals, a dog tax, a law requiring residents to use 'fly-traps,' and the prohibition of 'flippers and slings' within town limits to protect birds from thoughtless youth. The women also outlawed foot races, horse races, ball games, and all 'noisy sports' on the Sabbath....These active women also arranged for the town cemetery to be surveyed and plotted, purchased lumber and had bridges built over town ditches, joined with Kanab's Irrigation Company and built a large dike to protect the town from flooding....Toward the end

---

[77] One of my favorite moments from the hit movie *Napoleon Dynamite* is when one of the extras is shown wearing a Kanab Cowboys T-shirt.
[78] Reeve has written numerous articles books about Utah history. Much of my understanding of the subject has come thanks to his impressive research.

of the board's term, Mayor Howard noted that prior to the women's election, nine-tenths of the townsfolk did not know who the members of the town board were. In contrast, she asserted, even the children know all the names of the female board, and they are discussed 'in every home for good or ill.'"[79]

In addition to the record-setting Kanab City Council, Utah was also the second state in the nation to grant women the right to vote. Utahn Martha Hughes Cannon became the first state senator in American history. You will soon be able to see her in the U.S. Capitol, as one of the state's two statues on display to the rest of the country.

At a time when Kanab women were not only voting but running their town's government, the 19th Amendment would not be passed for another eight years giving women the right to vote nationwide.

Unfortunately this legacy of activism has not held over time in Utah. Women have not held political power in nearly as high of numbers as other states. It's time our state return to its roots and remember the Kanab City Council Rule. It's time for women to lead.

---

[79] Paul Reeve, "Kanab Residents Chose Women to Run Their Town in 1912." *History* Blazer, April 1995.

THE FOXLEY PRINCIPLE

Everyone in politics needs a good mentor.

No politico has done a better job helping younger Utahns find a path to their future professional success than Doug Foxley. For students looking to get more involved in Utah politics, their journey often begins with the always-colorful lobbyist. Unsurprisingly, his protégés end up doggedly loyal for decades to come.

It is appropriate that Utah State University named its weekly political lecture after the longtime university booster. The legendary lobbyist even teaches his own campaign management class to aspiring students at the University of Utah.

Whether you are a young student, or an older Utahn looking to get involved in politics, be sure to remember the Foxley Principle. Seek out a political mentor.[80] They can be tremendously helpful in navigating the state's political scene, which can at times seem confusing and even counterintuitive. All of us have more to learn and turning to longtime experts will be incredibly beneficial to your political future.

---

[80] The honorable mention name for this theory comes from the University of Utah legend J.D. Williams, who long-time political expert Pat Shea once called, "The Mount Rushmore of intellectual inquiry in Utah."* The influence of Williams was felt over his 40 years of teaching at the university, guiding generations of Utah politicians from both sides of the political spectrum.
*Twila Van Leer, "University of Utah political professor, mentor J.D. Williams dies." *Deseret News*, 5 September 2007.

THE QUESTIONNAIRE WARNING

Signing pledges will box you into future political positions.

The moment you announce your candidacy for a legislative or higher office, you will begin receiving questionnaires from numerous organizations. This includes many that you never knew existed. Such organizations will frequently threaten you with embarrassment if you refuse to fill out the survey. There are so many that any candidate filling them all out wouldn't have any time left over to actually campaign.

The purpose of these multitudinous questionnaires is to lock candidates into positions in perpetuity. Rather than answer every policy position, it is much better to outline key principles that will help guide your future decision-making.

Candidates regularly find themselves boxed into positions with little room to negotiate in the day-to-day grind of politics. Be direct with your constituents about where you stand on the issues of the day, but also maintain flexibility to manage the issues of tomorrow that will inevitably come your way.[81]

Avoid these interest-group pledges in all but the most important situations.

---

[81] An unfortunate trick from the consultant playbook is to dress up weak or vague policy positions with strong adjectives. It makes the candidate appear firm, without actually taking any position. This is easy to spot if you're looking for it and not recommended for successful elected leaders. Preserving flexibility for future decisions should never mean that you won't take strong stands.

THE HERBERT PRINCIPLE

Local government is the best training ground for Utah politicians.

Perhaps due to White Horse Fever, many prospective political candidates look in the mirror and immediately view themselves as a member of Congress or governor. But very rarely would they ever consider running for their local city council or county commission. Not Gary Herbert.

The third-longest serving governor in Utah history, Governor Herbert first served as a Utah County Commissioner for 14 years.[82] Many aspiring politicos could not stand 14 months as county commissioner before the grind of the job would wear them down. Yet those very same individuals frequently ponder a future congressional run or other prominent assignments.

Herbert himself admits that his journey into politics was quite improbable. "I was bashful and shy. I didn't even run for homeroom president. So, for a lot of people I grew up with when I became governor think, 'Wow, how did that happen?'"

And yet, Utahns continue to give the governor some of the highest approval ratings in the nation.

If you aren't willing to put in the time to do the difficult, unnoticed work of local politics, chances are you won't enjoy the often mundane work that comes with being governor or a member of Congress. Learn the Gary Herbert Rule of Utah politics and spend the evening with your local city council to better understand how to make your community a better place. Despite its lack of public attention, local government has more of an impact on your everyday life than any other political body.

---

[82] When Herbert finishes his current term, he will have become the second-longest serving governor in Utah history behind Governor Cal Rampton.

THE PATTI EDWARDS RULE

A supportive spouse is critical in any political race.

Patti Edwards, wife of longtime BYU football coach LaVell Edwards, wrote a regular sports column for the *Daily Herald* at the same time that her husband coached the team. Because of her role with the newspaper and membership in the Football Writers Association, she was given credentials to attend postgame press conferences with other reporters.

After a 31-10 loss to UCLA in the 1986 Freedom Bowl, she attended the postgame press conference with UCLA football coach Terry Donahue. Upset about a UCLA halfback pass late in the game with the team far ahead, she asked Donahue, "Do you really think it was kosher, running that halfback thing, with the score the way it was?"

Donahue tried to explain the play call, but as Edwards exited the room, she reportedly said, "I made my point." The resulting media frenzy would reach the *Los Angeles Times*, *Newsweek* and *Sports Illustrated* among many other publications.

An election can be an enormously trying time for any family. The ups and downs of a campaign will try even the most successful of marriages. If you are married, your spouse's support will be critical to your eventual success.[83]

---

[83] Special props go out to Governor Cal Rampton who got into an altercation with a leader of the John Birch Society who according to Rampton, "practically implied that [my wife] was a Communist."*

*Calvin L. Rampton, Floyd A. O'Neil, and Gregory C. Thompson, *As I Recall* (Salt Lake City: University of Utah Press, 1989), 192-3

A SUNDIATA GAINES MOMENT

Sometimes the most memorable moments come from the most unlikely of characters.

Undrafted out of college and uninvited to a single NBA training camp, Sundiata Gaines played abroad in Europe before signing a contract with the NBA's D-League Idaho Stampede. When Utah Jazz starting point guard Deron Williams[84] suffered a wrist injury, the Jazz called up Gaines from the D-League and signed him to a 10-day contract.

On the last day before his contract expired, the Jazz hosted the heavily favored Cleveland Cavaliers. With Williams out of the game and Lebron James scoring 20 points in the fourth quarter, the Jazz had one final possession, down 96-94. Ronnie Price tried to create an opening, but with only two seconds left on the game clock he desperately passed the ball to Gaines,[85] who quickly released the shot at the buzzer while falling to the ground. The shot was all net, the first three-pointer in his NBA career.

The next day the team would extend his contract, ultimately signing him for the rest of the season. Despite his short tenure and limited role on the team, Jazz fans will always remember Sundiata Gaines for that one glorious moment played over and over again in team highlight videos.

In politics, you may never know when your opportunity will arrive. For some people, even from the unlikeliest of places, they get one moment and only one moment to make their mark. Be prepared.

---

[84] I became a lifetime fan of Deron Williams when he complained to the *New York Post* about finding a school for his children following his trade to the Brooklyn Nets. He said, "The process of getting them into school is a nightmare. Even private schools where you pay are an ordeal. In Utah, you just send your kids to the first public school in the area because they're all great."

[85] I'm sure there is a political equivalent to the teammate who tosses you the ball with almost no time left on the shot clock. Playing political hot potato is certainly a reality.

THE AMBASSADOR CLUB RULE

Do your best to eliminate challengers before they ever run.

In the 1962 election, Cal Rampton wanted to run against incumbent U.S. Senator Wallace Bennett. The problem was that Rampton wasn't the only Democrat looking to challenge Bennett, with rumors that Congressman David King was also considering the same race.

That spring Rampton invited King to lunch at the Ambassador Club to discuss the election.[86] As Rampton recalls the meeting, "We sat there talking and trying to jockey each other out of position. I told him that I was going to run, and he said he hadn't made up his mind whether he would. I told him I would run whether or not he did, hoping that would convince him not to run. Finally, however, we both filed for the Democratic nomination."[87]

While it might be one of the more awkward meetings of your life, sitting down face to face with your potential opponent can be immensely valuable. You may not succeed in managing them out of the race, but it is certainly worth the effort, especially in intra-party races.

---

[86] The Ambassador Club was built in 1885 by the federal government as a home for women escaping polygamy. It would later be turned into a social club frequented by non-Mormon businessman. A gambling operation was raided there in 1960 by Salt Lake City Police Chief Cleon Skousen. Mayor J. Bracken Lee was at the club at the time of the raid, which some Skousen supporters pointed to when Lee controversially fired the police chief.
[87] Calvin L. Rampton, Floyd A. O'Neil, and Gregory C. Thompson, *As I Recall* (Salt Lake City: University of Utah Press, 1989), 112.

THE BUD SCRUGGS COROLLARY

Elections are often won before a single ballot is ever cast.

One of the most entertaining leaders in Utah political history is Bud Scruggs, former chief of staff to Governor Norm Bangerter. Prior to his appointment, Scruggs led the reelection efforts of U.S. Senators Jake Garn and Orrin Hatch. Joking at the time that he proved his abilities by pulling the campaigns "out of the fire," Scruggs was always good with the self-deprecating one-liner.[88]

Perhaps his most incredible political success was navigating the 2016 reelection for U.S. Senator Mike Lee. With several prominent leaders of the business community actively looking for a challenger to Lee, Scruggs led an outreach effort to these same business leaders to convince them to back off their campaign. Through the Scruggs efforts and significant work by Senator Lee, the incumbent skated into the general election without a primary opponent.

In politics, we refer to this phase of the campaign as the invisible primary. Campaign forces may not be fighting on the front pages of the local newspaper, but there is a significant amount of work going on behind the scenes to marshal support and eliminate opponents.[89]

Like Scruggs, some of the most astute campaign experts are those who are able to convince potential opponents and their supporters to never

[88] One of my favorite Scruggs stories comes from a practical joke he played on a Republican friend. During the 2016 presidential election, he found an outdoor apron online that said, "Grillary Clinton" on it. Purchasing the product, he was shocked to find out that the apron was sold by the official Hillary Clinton for President campaign and, therefore, Scruggs was named as a donor to her campaign in public records.
[89] Former legislator Steve Urquhart briefly filed to run against U.S. Senator Orrin Hatch in his 2006 reelection. Urquhart struggled to meet his fundraising goals with the Hatch campaign actively working against him, ultimately dropping out of the race before the convention.*
*One of Hatch's biggest critics in that race was Dallas Mavericks owner Mark Cuban, who called the senior Senator "the digital Joe McCarthy" for his work to prevent music piracy.

mount a run in the first place. It sounds easy enough, but when egos are involved, this is anything but simple. It takes a unique personality with a deft touch.

If this fails, cutting off your opponent's supply lines (e.g. fundraising, key supporters and grassroots volunteers) is the next course of action.[90] The more isolated a candidate feels, the more likely they are to not move forward in the election.

Thanks to the Bud Scruggs Corollary, most serious challenges are ended before they ever seriously begin.

---

[90] Referred to as a Mussolini Moment, make sure that if you are going to oppose someone's candidacy you are prepared to go all the way.

THE JIM HANSEN PRINCIPLE

Get involved because you have a cause, not because you want a job.

That line is a direct quote from U.S. Congressman Jim Hansen, according to former staffer and future gubernatorial chief of staff, Justin Harding. "Get involved because you have a cause, not because you want a job."[91]

Harding recalls that Hansen first became engaged in politics because he wanted to help fix Farmington's water system. For years, anyone who listened to a Congressman Hansen speech heard about the Farmington water saga.[92]

The first question any good campaign consultant will ask you is, "Why do you want to run?" If you don't have an immediate answer to that question, you may want to pause and reevaluate your potential candidacy. Adding a line to your résumé isn't sufficient. Serving in a prominent position in your community won't cut it. You need a reason to run.

Learn the Jim Hansen Rule and find a cause. Otherwise, your time in public office will be far less meaningful.

---

[91] LaVarr Webb, "Utah Policy Genius Panel: Mentors Who Made a Difference," *Utah Policy*, 15 May 2016.

[92] During his time in Congress, Hansen championed Hill Air Force Base and many important public lands measures as chair of the House Natural Resources Committee. Perhaps in his most popular legislative effort, Hansen helped eliminate the controversial 55 mile per hour national speed limit, originally passed in order to combat the 1970s energy crisis. The Double Nickel Rule is named in honor of this legislation, reminding us that well-intentioned legislation is frequently riddled with unintended consequences.

THE DIXIE LEAVITT PRINCIPLE

Be kind and fair to everyone, no matter how unimportant they may seem.

When Governor Mike Leavitt was appointed to President George W. Bush's administration, his U.S. Senate confirmation was surprisingly aided by Democratic Senate Minority Whip Harry Reid. During the back-and-forth questioning of Leavitt, Reid asked if he could make a comment about the nomination. Rather than criticize the Republican Leavitt, Reid went on to share a very personal story about Leavitt's father, Dixie.

The following is Senator Reid's comments about his experience with the elder Leavitt:

"When I thought I was an athlete, I went to school at a college in southern Utah, that is where his father was an insurance salesman. When my wife and I decided we were going to get married between my sophomore and junior year in college, I went to Mr. Leavitt and I said I would like to buy an insurance policy and I want to make sure it covers maternity in case we have a baby. A couple of years later we had a baby and the insurance policy didn't cover maternity. By then I had moved to a different school hundreds of miles away, so I called his father and said, do you remember selling this insurance policy to me and he said yes. I am not sure he remembered, but I said I bought it because I wanted maternity and it doesn't have any. He said, did I do that? I said, yes. He said, well send me the bill. I sent him the bill and he paid them. I don't think that happens very often, so I have always had a great affection for the Leavitt family as a result of that."[93]

---

[93] *Nomination of Governor Michael O. Leavitt, of Utah, to be Administrator, U.S. Environmental Protection Agency: Hearing Before the Committee on Environment and Public Works,* U.S. Senate, 108th Congress, September 23, 2003.

With that short anecdote having been shared from decades earlier, Governor Leavitt's nomination moved forward quickly and he was easily confirmed by the Senate.[94] One small act of business integrity by his father 50 years earlier to an unknown student would dramatically impact his son's position in one of the highest political positions in the country.

Never cut corners in your personal or professional dealings. People have a habit of remembering.

---

[94] One of the aides Leavitt brought with him to Washington was the brilliant Rich McKeown who would serve as chief of staff to Leavitt at the U.S. Environmental Protection Agency and Department of Health and Human Services. The two long-time partners continue to work together today at Leavitt Partners and even co-authored an excellent book titled *Finding Allies, Building Alliances: 8 Elements That Bring and Keep People Together.*

THE MICHAEL DOLEAC RULE

Some people are late bloomers.

When University of Utah Coach Rick Majerus visited Michael Doleac's high school team, the future basketball star only played three minutes the entire game. Doleac had been cut as a freshman and barely made the team the following year. As a junior, Doleac was the last man off the bench with no expectation of a future in high school basketball, let alone college.

When Majerus surprisingly offered Doleac a scholarship, the future star had never started a single high school basketball game. Doleac said, "I didn't really even know what a scholarship was when he made the offer....You have to remember that during most of high school I rarely even played. I never expected to go to college to play basketball. When it happened, it was a complete surprise."[95]

Doleac would go on to lead the Utes to the national championship game and be drafted 12th overall in the 1998 NBA Draft.[96]

Political fates can change very quickly. Governor Gary Herbert was a shy high school student who was never considered for any high school elected office. However, he would later go on to serve as one of Utah's most successful governors.

Some are youthful prodigies who are immediately successful in whatever they do. Others need a little experience first before ultimately succeeding far more than anyone ever imagined.

---

[95] Rick Majerus, *My Life on a Napkin: Pillow Mints, Playground Dreams, and Coaching the Runnin Utes.* (New York: Hyperion, 2000), 87.
[96] At the conclusion of his 10-year NBA career, Doleac returned to the University of Utah where he earned a master's degree in physics. Today, he teaches at Park City High School and coaches the boys' basketball team.

If success doesn't come to you quickly, be patient and remember the Michael Doleac Rule. Sometimes the very best leaders just need a little time to grow into the role.

CHAPTER 2

ELECTION STRATEGY

THE NATALIE GOCHNOUR RULE

Every campaign needs an overarching narrative.

One of Utah's leading public policy experts is Natalie Gochnour, the director of the Kem Gardner Policy Institute at the University of Utah. An economist by background, Gochnour is one of the most sought after speakers on Utah issues thanks in no small part to the insightful analysis she always provides.

In many ways, I consider Gochnour to be the chief storyteller of the state. She understands the key issues that Utah residents are encountering and has the unique ability to emotionally connect with diverse audiences. Every time I hear her speak, I leave with a fresh perspective on the state.

When running a campaign, it is critical that you establish the key narrative of your candidacy. Why are you running and what do you hope to accomplish? Those who don't become easily distracted with whatever the news cycle of the day may be.

Remember the Gochnour Rule and develop your own campaign narrative. Without it, even the best candidates will struggle.

THE BECKY LOCKHART THEORY

Utahns like underdogs. Underestimate them at your own peril.

It is appropriate that Utah's first female Speaker of the House would be elected in an improbable campaign that shocked political experts across the state. She ultimately prevailed by only one vote against the heavily favored incumbent speaker.

One of a victorious speaker's chief tools is the ability to grant committee assignments to other members. An adversarial relationship can lead to two years on committees that are unimportant to your district. The risk was significant, but Representative Becky Lockhart took the chance and emerged victorious.

As Speaker of the House, she would lead an unprecedented investigation into potential impeachment proceedings against the sitting attorney general in 2013. Looking back at the subsequent events, this particular course of action might seem commonsensical, but at the time it was anything but the safe course of action.

In Utah, we love a good underdog.[1] We feel like underdogs in comparison to other states. Members of the Church of Jesus Christ of Latter-day Saints feel like a minority faith. Non-Mormons feel like underdogs in a state dominated by the majority religion.

Several years after her passing, Lockhart's husband Stan shared a quote from Becky that helps explain her motives for pushing forward in the face of adversity:

"Using your real voice might make you uncomfortable. It might make the people around you feel uncomfortable, but until we make it normal for women to be heard, until we are heard for our ideas and not viewed as

---

[1] See the Matheson Corollary (p. 35).

tokens, that's the price we'll pay. I for one, have been willing to pay that price."[2]

Everybody loves a good underdog. And the act of overcoming great odds adds even more to the narrative of unexpected greatness.[3] Nobody thought Becky Lockhart would be Utah's first female Speaker of the House. However, as you walk through the beautiful Capitol complex, you will find her name on the prestigious House building.

Remember Speaker Lockhart if you ever doubt yourself. It might be difficult at first, but Utahns love to rally behind a good underdog.

---

[2] Another favorite quote from Speaker Lockhart, "If you hear anyone say, 'This is really a very simple bill,' that should be your first warning."
[3] The lopsided conflict somehow makes the underdog that much more memorable.

THE LEE GREENWOOD THEORY

Be understated. Over-the-top displays are poorly received.

At the 1992 Republican state convention, U.S. Senate candidate Joe
Cannon delivered a surprise with the unannounced appearance of
country music legend Lee Greenwood singing his popular song, "God
Bless the U.S.A." As the song played, a large American flag was unfurled
behind him. Some in the crowd responded enthusiastically, singing along
with the star. However, many others felt like the appearance was
completely over the top.[4]

In many ways, personal wealth can present a double-edged sword for a
potential candidate. Running a campaign without any money is
impossible.[5] However, there is not only a law of diminishing returns when
it comes to campaign spending, there is also a point where more spending
can actually be adversarial to a candidate's success.

Joe Cannon was immediately perceived to be the favorite in the race with
everyone else hoping to come in second at convention. The advantages of
Cannon's independent wealth, however, proved to be part of his demise.
In one internal campaign memo from his victorious opponent, an adviser
suggested the campaign should strive to make Cannon look like a "rich
kid trying to buy an election."

In reality, the winner Bob Bennett spent nearly as much as Cannon on the
race, without the same kind of adversarial views towards his spending.
Perception is everything. Simpler is better in Utah politics.

---

[4] Such theatrics can often feel excessive, but one of my favorite convention traditions is
affectionately referred to as "Sign Wars."* Campaign workers line up to race against rival
campaigns to get the best sign locations.
[5] Many candidates have failed while thinking that their campaign will somehow be "different."
It almost never is. You need money to win an election.
*And rumors of Sign Wars.

THE HORIUCHI HAZMAT COROLLARY

Over-the-top gestures can work if it's obvious the person is in on the joke.

As chairman of the Utah Democratic Party, Randy Horiuchi stepped out to a press conference in the 1992 U.S. Senate race wearing a full Hazmat suit. His reasoning for the unique outfit was the need to protect himself from the toxic chemicals released by the Bennett Paint Company and the Republican nominee for U.S. Senate Bob Bennett.

The media covered the event, and Republicans and Democrats alike all laughed at the gag.

Decades later at a memorial service honoring the recently passed Horiuchi, fellow council member Michael Jensen stepped to the microphone to deliver remarks in honor of his former colleague. To the surprise and delight of the audience, Jensen came forward dressed in a full Hazmat suit in honor of his good friend.

In many ways, the over-the-top press conference became the calling card for Horiuchi. His most legendary moments always came with a prop: the Hazmat suit, fishing waders or a dirty kitchen sink. No hyperbole was off limits with Horiuchi, and much of his political success could be attributed to his unique brand of politics.

Utahns have a sense of humor, and Horiuchi was the king of landing a joke in the Beehive state.[6]

---

[6] One of the best campaign ads in Utah politics came in his successful 1990 race against incumbent Tom Shimuzu: "Why would you want an old Shimizu when you can have a new Horiuchi?"

THE GAIL MILLER RULE

Be down to earth. Shop at Costco.

No one in Utah is more beloved than Gail Miller. To serve as a baseline for popularity, Dan Jones frequently polled her name alongside politicians and other prominent Utahns. No one polls higher than her, one of Utah's greatest success stories.

But it wasn't always that way. Growing up in Salt Lake City's Marmalade District on Quince Street, she never had central heating or air conditioning during her entire childhood. She said of this time, "It wasn't unusual for me to go to school with holes in my socks and underwear. Motivated to solve that embarrassing problem, I learned to sew my own clothes by the time I was in the fourth grade."[7]

Today, she is now the owner of the one of the largest privately-owned businesses in the entire United States. And yet, she's still the same Gail Miller that she was growing up on Quince Street. The money never changed her. She has her own garden, cans her own fruit, irons and sews, and shops at Costco right along with the rest of us.

Utahns appreciate someone who is down to earth, no matter how successful they have been in their private lives.[8]

---

[7] Gail Miller and Jason F. Wright. *Courage to Be You: Inspiring Lessons from an Unexpected Journey* (Salt Lake City, UT: Deseret Book, 2018), 42.

[8] Another example that deserves recognition is former Utah Jazz Coach Jerry Sloan. Each summer, Sloan would return to his family farm in southern Illinois. His unpretentious Midwestern style always resonated well with Utahns.

THE PHIL HANSEN COROLLARY

Be especially frugal with taxpayer funds.

As with other statewide elected officials, former Utah Attorney General Phil Hansen was provided with a state vehicle in 1965 at taxpayers' expense. This alone wouldn't be an issue. However, Hansen's choice of a Jaguar didn't win him many friends in the court of public opinion.

Hansen's defense was that the Jaguar would actually resale at a higher price and, therefore, save taxpayers money. I don't think anyone in the state bought the narrative.

Serving for only one term, the Phil Hansen Corollary is a reminder for all Utah elected officials. Taxpayer funds are limited, and the quickest way to anger voters is to spend recklessly on items viewed as personal in nature.

THE CAP FERRY PRINCIPLE

When coupled with a humble personality, don't be afraid to stand out.

Former Senate President Miles "Cap" Ferry was legendary for his choice of clothing, including a red plaid tuxedo. On the day budget figures were to be released, he would wear an oversized tie covered in dollar signs.

In a state that traditionally shuns flamboyance, the rules didn't seem to apply to Ferry. Most attribute this to his humble personality that could have seemed so at odds with his choice of clothing. Former Speaker of the House Nolan Karras said of Ferry, "He wasn't a showoff. He got things done because he was so approachable."[9]

Being a little unique goes a long way in Utah politics. We especially appreciate it from those not trying to steal attention away from everyone else.[10] Ferry developed a reputation as being a quiet leader who was willing to work in a bipartisan manner.

If you are too flamboyant, you can come across as annoying and self-indulgent. However, if you can strike the balance of being humble and unique, you will find that others respect you as someone who is both approachable and memorable. [11]

---

[9] Paul Rolly, "Former Utah Senate, farming boss 'Cap' Ferry dies: colleagues recall him as a 'quiet' leader, loud dresser." *Salt Lake Tribune*, 4 April 2017.

[10] Another great example of this principle was longtime Utah Jazz Assistant Coach Phil Johnson. Always humble and never one to steal attention, Johnson's choice of a personal pet bobcat always fascinated those who came to visit his home.

[11] Ferry and his wife Sue left behind a legacy of some of the brightest political minds in the state, including grandchildren David and Justin Stewart, Representative Joel Ferry, former Representative Ben Ferry and grandson-in-law Senate Majority Whip Dan Hemmert.

THE AGENDA 21 RULE

Be careful of those with hidden agendas.

I like to use the phrase "Agenda 21" as a misnomer for someone having a hidden agenda. For example, "I don't trust that lobbyist. I just feel like she has an Agenda 21 on this one."

The first time I ran for public office, I entered a Republican delegate's home where we talked about several issues I felt were important in the race. Towards the end of the conversation, the delegate turned to me and asked, "But where do you stand on Agenda 21?" I drew a blank.

It turns out Agenda 21 is a conspiracy theory focused on the alleged secret efforts to eliminate U.S. sovereignty and institute United Nations rule across the country.[12] I would soon find out this delegate was not alone in his concerns, as I heard the same question several times in my visits to delegate homes.

Sometimes in your first experience in public office, you will find certain individuals anxious to help. Only later will you discover that they might have ulterior motives for their assistance.

Beware the Agenda 21's.

---

[12] No, I was not campaigning in La Verkin at the time, home to Utah's only U.N. free zone.

THE DIANE STEWART RULE

Opening your home to others helps to break down barriers.

Recently called "the grand dame of Utah politics"[13] by a local news network, Diane Stewart and her husband Sam have hosted some of the most prominent names in national politics at their Salt Lake City home. The Stewarts have welcomed former President George Bush, Governors Gary Herbert and Jon Huntsman, Chelsea Clinton and too many others to name here. If a gathering place needed to be found, the Stewarts quickly volunteered to help.

During the 2009 debate on a LGBT non-discrimination ordinance in Salt Lake City, the Stewart home was the neutral meeting grounds for representatives from the Church of Jesus Christ of Latter-day Saints and leaders of the LGBT community. That historic meeting planted the seeds for a relationship that would allow future collaborations between the two groups, including a statewide non-discrimination law in 2015.

And none of it would have occurred, unless Stewart had been willing to open up her home for the discussion. In politics, there can be great power in holding events. Meeting together can lead to greater understanding and potential collaboration, even among the most strident of opponents.

---

[13] Chris Jones, "Avenues home is a political powerhouse." *KUTV*, 21 March 2016.

THE JACKRABBIT RULE

Don't make fun of Utahns. They have long memories.

In the 1972 election, Salt Lake businessman Nicolas Strike challenged incumbent Governor Cal Rampton in the gubernatorial race. Strike struggled, in part due a mistake he made when criticizing the popular Rampton for spending state dollars on an interstate highway in southern Utah, where Strike indicated no one lived but jackrabbits.[14]

In the process of that short exchange, the candidate managed to alienate much of his base of support in rural Utah (a Republican stronghold) and was easily defeated 70-30 percent in the general election.

What might make a good talking point with one audience may come back to bite you with another. Don't offend Utahns. They won't soon forget it.

---

[14] While this slip of tongue was unfortunate, Strike should be remembered for his tremendous contributions to the state, including his time as parish president of the Holy Trinity Greek Orthodox Church. Strike was a tireless defender of the Greek community and worked throughout his life to make sure the Greek culture would be remembered in the Beehive State.

THE KARRAS THANK YOU CARD RULE

Be conservative when counting votes.

A story is told among Utah politicos about former Utah Speaker of the House Nolan Karras,[15] the gifted leader who subsequently ran for governor in 2004.[16]

Legislators are given only one secret ballot during their time in office: leadership votes. All other votes are public record. As a result, the process can be almost impossible to predict. After emerging victorious in a leadership election in the 1989 Legislature, Karras joked he now needed to write 37 thank-you notes for the 31 votes he received.[17] Even he didn't know who didn't follow through with their commitment to vote for him.

This counting problem is especially prevalent in the conflict-averse political climate found in the state. Voters are more likely to give the impression they will support a candidate, when in reality the opposing candidate came away with the very same impression. The voter may have felt like they were simply being nice to both candidates without being deceitful in any way.

As a result, a margin must be built into every campaign plan when dealing with secret ballots. This is especially true in smaller elections such as party conventions where a secret ballot has typically been granted to delegates.

Learn the Nolan Karras Thank You Card Rule. The difference between a good politician and a bad one is how well you can count.

---

[15] Karras has been one of Utah's most exceptional minds. His ascent to power at such a young age was no coincidence.

[16] His campaign manager was the brilliant Steve Starks (age 27 at the time), the future president of Larry H. Miller Sports & Entertainment.

[17] Having heard the story several times (with different numbers), legislative records indicate there were 48 Republicans in the 1989 Legislature, meaning Karras would have needed at least 25 votes from his peers.

THE DORÉ-ECCLES RULE

The smallest decisions can have the biggest impacts.

Take a stroll around almost any college campus, and you will see their names, George S. and Dolores Doré Eccles. Visit any community event, and almost always it would not occur without the support of this incredibly generous Utah family. In my small county of Sanpete, the opportunities provided by this family are truly breathtaking.[18] However, far too few Utahns know much about who these titans of business and community were.

Born to the self-made man David Eccles,[19] two brothers George and Marriner Eccles formed the multi-state bank, First Security Corporation.[20] George would run the remarkably successful business for 48 years, while Marriner went on to become chairman of the Federal Reserve Board during the Great Depression.[21]

George and his wife Dolores, known as Lolie to her friends, would lead the family's philanthropic efforts, focusing on the arts, education and many other social causes. Without these two together, Utah would struggle to provide many of the educational and cultural opportunities that exist today.

---

[18] Cleone Peterson Eccles was born in Fairview, Utah and her love for the county was evident throughout her life.

[19] I cannot recommend enough the Leonard Arrington book, *David Eccles: Pioneer Western Industrialist*. The David Eccles story is far too important to try and tell in a footnote.

[20] They give 110 percent.

[21] There is a statue of Marriner Eccles at the Utah State Capitol complex. One day I recall looking out from my office window and seeing a man in a suit all alone pausing to look at the statue. The man drew close and slowly wiped some mark or dirt from the shoes of the legendary Marriner Eccles. He paused again, before eventually departing. As he turned around, I immediately recognized the man as Spencer F. Eccles, the former CEO of First Security Corporation and nephew to Marriner Eccles.

And yet, their chance meeting might not have ever happened had it not been for a teacher's simple decision on seating assignments. When the two attended college together from completely different parts of the country and different social circles, fate would have it that the teacher assigned students to sit in alphabetical order with Dolores Doré seated next to George Eccles.

Had the two been assigned to different seats or different classes, think how different Utah might be today. Recent estimates indicate that between 15 and 20 percent of all philanthropic giving in the state comes from one family: the Eccles. In the last 50 years, this gracious Utah family has given more than $1 billion to Utah charitable organizations. While the family has various foundations, much of the financial support for these charitable contributions comes from the George S. and Dolores Doré Eccles Foundation, having given more than $500 million to so many different efforts in the Beehive State.

In a campaign, you will have thousands of decisions to make, many of them frequently minor in nature. But never underestimate the importance of these seemingly unimportant decisions. Sometimes it is the smallest of moments that can leave the most lasting of impacts.

THE IRON COUNTY SECRET

Some disregarded voters are more important than you think.

For nearly half of the last 40 years (1977-2017), Utah was led by governors who claimed small communities in rural Iron County as their hometowns.[22] Scott Matheson (Parowan)[23] and Mike Leavitt (Cedar City) both embraced their rural backgrounds to their political advantage.[24]

The latest Census Bureau tells us that more than 90 percent of Utahns live in urban areas, the eighth most urban state in the nation. In all, Utahns only live on 1.1 percent of the state's entire land mass.[25] This leads most political consultants to dismiss the importance of rural Utah in a statewide race. But digging deeper into the data tells a very different story.

First and foremost, rural voters frequently participate in elections in significantly higher numbers than their urban peers. As any consultant knows, the key is not your numbers in an overall poll. The number of likely voters in the contested election is much more telling.

---

[22] Credit should probably be given to Old Sorrel on this one.
[23] Parowan is affectionately known as the Mother Town of southern Utah. I highly recommend you attend the annual Parowan birthday celebration held each year on January 13.
[24] Mike Leavitt's farmer-themed commercials in 1992 were especially brilliant.
[25] This discrepancy in land mass to population was demonstrated during a failed Japanese attack in World War II. An estimated 9,000 hydrogen balloons were launched from Japan with an intended target of the western United States (fewer than 300 would make it). The balloons each carried five bombs set to activate upon impact with the ground. The campaign largely failed due to detonation in mostly rural areas far from urban population centers. Five known bombs were reported in Utah (Box Elder, Duchesne and Iron Counties) with no reported injuries. Local law enforcement was notified by the FBI who wanted to retrieve an undetonated balloon for additional analysis. Former Box Elder County Sheriff Warren Hyde received a call about one balloon floating nearby. He raced to the spot and chased after the balloon, eventually grabbing a shroud line where he spent the next 45 minutes floating up and down before successfully tethering it to the ground. I love the image of Utah's longest-serving sheriff (32 years) floating in the sky hanging on to a Japanese hydrogen balloon bomb before wrestling it to the ground unharmed.

At present, Utah almost always votes for Republicans in statewide races. Attorney General Jan Graham in 1992 was the last Democrat elected statewide. This means that the most critical election is almost always the Republican primary election.

In these GOP primary elections, instead of representing only 10 percent of the voting bloc, the percentage of rural voters is significantly higher (20-25 percent) in nearly every recent contested election. To put that into perspective, rural Utah has accounted for more votes than Utah County in every GOP primary election since 2000.

Every political consultant will advise you to focus on Utah County but very few make much of an effort in rural Utah. Of course, it goes without saying that very few political consultants have set foot in rural Utah besides a pit stop in Scipio on the way down to St. George.[26]

A person running from a rural base of support would start off with almost an identical position as someone from Utah County or the Davis-Weber area. Counterintuitively as the number of total voters increase, the percentage of rural voters is not diluted and, in some cases, even increases.

Longtime historian Ross Peterson called this phenomenon part of his three G's of Utah politics: geography, genealogy and God.[27] It is critical that you understand the rivalries in the communities you intend to serve. The issues of geography can be statewide, but they can also be found within an individual community. Some of the most important voters can be found in areas that were previously ignored by other candidates.

---

[26] For the political consultants making the trek, I recommend the Scipio Petting Zoo.
[27] Peterson is likely my all-time favorite person to hear give a speech. He is a gifted orator and one of the most respected historians in the Intermountain West. Utah should feel fortunate that we poached him away from his native southern Idaho for so many years.

THE REVERSE DOG YEAR RULE

People expect a little local flavor, especially in rural Utah.

I heard one prominent politician from rural Utah compare living in rural Utah to the opposite of how we count dog years. New arrivals who came to town 20 years ago really only have been here for three years thanks to the rural Utah Reverse Dog Year Rule.

In many ways, a rural upbringing can be tremendously valuable in a political race on the Wasatch Front. However, the reverse isn't true. If you want to run for office in rural Utah, you better have a 435-area code on your phone.[28]

One exception to this rule is if you have family ancestry from the area. You could move away or have never lived in the community, but that one family tie makes the Reverse Dog Year Rule no longer in force.

---

[28] I have been the victim of vandalism only once in my life. When parked overnight in Salt Lake City, someone spray-painted the numbers "801" on my vehicle. As a native of rural Utah, I can't think of a more offensive gesture.

THE KMTI RULE

You may be surprised where voters get their information.

Growing up in Sanpete County, my family had the constant background noise of the local radio station KMTI AM 650 on every morning. While eating breakfast or getting ready for the day, I could hear the deep voice of Doug Barton telling the news in our little county. It turns out, my experience wasn't unique.[29]

As a county commissioner years later, I would participate in a regular radio segment called "Table Talk" on KMTI. Sandwiched between the local funeral report and "Tradio,"[30] I was convinced no one ever heard my reports. Then I would go to the local grocery store, the post office or anywhere else. Wherever I went, I always heard the same thing. "Nice job on the radio today." I was amazed. It seemed like people were always listening to the radio.

In his come-from-behind 1992 U.S. Senate victory, Senator Bob Bennett credited a last-minute surge in rural counties for his victory. Weeks before the election, a Bennett consultant stated the following in an internal campaign memo: "Cannon dominates Bennett in the rural areas on every important matter in the poll. Overall, Cannon wins 60 to 26 percent in the rural counties, a 34 point advantage there." The last-minute push by Bennett in rural Utah turned the tide in his favor. Cannon did win the rural vote, but only by a single-digit margin of victory.

---

[29] KMTI, named for its headquarters in Manti, can now be heard on air in 16 of Utah's 29 counties.
[30] The program "Tradio" consists of a radio announcer reading classified ads over the air for 8-10 minutes at a time. "Red Heifer found in Spring City. Approximately 800 pounds with an ear marker but no brand. If she's yours, call Dell Jensen at 469-0296.*
*This was from an actual ad from "Tradio" on the same day I wrote this chapter. If you still haven't found your heifer, give Dell a call.

Senator Bennett recalled the campaign's strategy in rural Utah. "I went into the radio studio and I recorded a 60-second radio spot just hammering on Wayne Owens." When the Democrat Owens confronted Bennett about the spot, he replied, "I have to win a primary. You are the most hated man in rural Utah. If I'm going to win the primary, I have to prove to them that I hate you more than Joe hates you." The response was immediate and overwhelming.[31] "That spot started to run, and our phones started to ring off the hook," Bennett said. "We spent all this money on television and none of these people had heard of me....Radio was the medium to reach rural Utah."[32]

You may get information from one source of media, but others may receive it from another. A campaign may assume that television ads will cover voters in all parts of the state but remember the KMTI Strategy. Not all Utahns get their information from the same place.[33]

---

[31]One campaign staffer recalled another important shift in rural strategy. "The Bennett camp took out ads in rural newspapers comparing Joe Cannon's spending on the Senate race to the annual budget for the particular county that paper appeared in," he said. These examples proved to be especially compelling in many of the counties where Cannon's spending exceeded the county budget. The ads stated that, "Cannon campaign expenditures exceed the operating budgets of more than half of Utah's counties." Rural voters responded positively to the attack. "When that hit, Joe's people went absolutely ballistic," Bennett said. The Cannon camp accused Bennett of going negative, but their argument only helped to reinforce the spending issue.*

[32]Bob Bennett, interview by author, 21 April 2011, Salt Lake City.

[33]A Bennett campaign consultant raised an important point regarding the issue of different campaign media in an internal campaign memo. "You can also be more direct in your attacks on Cannon on radio than you can on TV," he said. "TV is a cool medium and does not take well to harsh conflict. Radio is a hot medium and can stand more fighting." Different types of media continue to emerge, but radio continues to have a lasting impact, especially in rural Utah.

*This is essence of the "I Am Not a Crook Rule," named after President Richard Nixon's famous comments. The more you deny something, the more likely you will reinforce the original attack in a voter's mind. The sooner you can move on, the better.

THE STATE STREET TACOS RULE

Be proactive to inoculate yourself from potential criticism.

One of Utah's most brilliant public leaders was former Governor Jon Huntsman Jr., a lodestar in the state's political history.

When he first ran for governor in 2004, he could have been criticized for his upbringing as the son of wealth. Instead Huntsman emphasized portions of his history that showed he was a regular person just like you and me.

He talked about his time playing the keyboard in a high school band. He mentioned meeting his wife at his job washing dishes at a local restaurant. He talked about his love for dirt bikes. He frequently quoted rock lyrics in political speeches. And of course, he made frequent stops at the taco cart on State Street in downtown Salt Lake City. To his credit, the stories never felt contrived for political benefit.

It is common for politicians to come across as out of touch. Huntsman pushed back against that narrative from the very beginning.

It is imperative that you come across as relatable in your political campaign. Voters often select the candidate they find most likeable, irrespective of their views on specific policies. The best way to prevent potential criticism is to not shy away from public contact. The more the public gets to know you, the harder it will be for others to criticize you.

Define yourself early, or risk being defined by your opponents in ways you may not like.

THE BILL ORTON AND HIS FAMILY PRINCIPLE

Utah voters punish candidates who go too negative.

Two days before the 1990 election, a local newspaper published a large ad paid for by the Utah Republican Party. On one side was Republican congressional candidate pictured with his large family and the caption, "Karl Snow and his family." Next to the photo was a picture of Democratic candidate Bill Orton, alone and unmarried with the caption, "Bill Orton and his family." Below both photos was the text, "Some candidates want you to believe that their personal values don't matter...Families do matter! Vote Republican."

Voters overwhelmingly rejected what was perceived to be a dirty attack on Orton's single background. Every Utah politico is familiar with this infamous ad, credited in large part for Snow's defeat by an astounding 22 percent in the heavily Republican district. Prominent pollster Dan Jones commented, "It went over with the public like a burp in church."[34]

Campaign consultants never seem to understand this simple rule in Utah politics. Residents of the Beehive State strongly dislike attacks on personal character and what they perceive to be unfair mudslinging. This mistake is habitually made by high-powered national consultants who have little to no experience in the Beehive State. Time and time again, more damage is done by these so-called experts when local Utahns could easily tell you the ad will immediately backfire.[35]

---

[34] U.S. Senator Orrin Hatch said at the time, "I've seen a lot of stupid things in politics, but this ad was the stupidest thing I've ever seen." Bob Bernick Jr., "Utah GOP Surveys Damage, Examines Options." *Deseret News*, 9 November 1990.

[35] Orton went on to serve three terms in Congress, before being defeated in 1996 by Chris Cannon. Many credit President Bill Clinton's last-minute designation of the Grand Staircase Escalante National Monument for Orton's defeat. In a story that has become legendary in Utah Republican circles, Clinton made the announcement in Arizona at the Grand Canyon without giving advance notice to Utah leaders, including Orton. Four years earlier, Clinton finished third in only one state (Utah) during the 1992 election.

THE NOVELTY RULE

Unfairly attacking your opponent will backfire.

During the 2012 Republican convention, most political observers expected no candidate in the newly created 4th Congressional District to receive more than the 60-percent threshold needed to avoid a primary fight. The conventional wisdom was that Representative Carl Wimmer and Saratoga Springs Mayor Mia Love would emerge from the field.

But then the "novelty" comment occurred.

Utah Attorney General Mark Shurtleff came to the microphone before the final round of balloting to announce his support of Wimmer. In that speech, he said, "You have to pick a person with a proven track record who can beat Jim Matheson this fall. Not a novelty." The response to Shurtleff's perceived attack on Love's race was immediate, and delegates were furious.[36]

Wimmer followed with his own speech, but it didn't matter. Love emerged victorious with 70.4 percent of the vote to Wimmer's 29.6 percent. Despite fewer candidates being in the race in the second round of balloting, Wimmer actually lost votes from his first round total of 31 percent. Later in the day, Shurtleff apologized to Love for the comment, but the race had already been lost.

Utahns are extremely sensitive to unfair attacks against other candidates. If you choose to engage in them, be prepared for the inevitable backlash.

---

[36] For all the criticism delegates receive, they should also get credit for pushing against such attacks. If you are going to criticize them for making decisions you disagree with, you also need to give them credit when you agree.

THE BUEHNER RULE

The best attacks use your opponent's own words against them.

During Utah Governor Cal Rampton's 1968 run for a second term, he faced former member of the Church of Jesus Christ of Latter-day Saint's Presiding Bishopric Carl W. Buehner.[37]

Perhaps the most memorable moment of the campaign occurred during one of the few debates in the race. Rampton mentioned a pledge Buehner had made to cut state expenditures by 30 percent and pressed him to specify what programs he would cut. Buehner denied ever making the 30-percent promise, to which Rampton responded live in the debate by playing an audio recording of Buehner making the pledge.[38]

The embarrassing moment crystallizes an important point in politics. With so much spin occurring between candidates and their supporters, it's often difficult to know who is telling the truth. If your opponent can make your point for you, there isn't any room for doubt.

---

[37] I am legally obligated to mention the middle initial of all LDS General Authorities.

[38] Buehner canceled the remaining debates after this incident, an issue that Rampton repeatedly drove home in his message to voters. There may be a corollary out there to the Jack Carlson Rule (p. 94) where skipping debates can hurt a candidate who is either (1) challenging an incumbent, or (2) previously accepted the debate invitation before canceling.

THE DEEP THROAT COROLLARY

Eliminate controversies immediately, ideally in your opponent's own words.

While the Buehner Rule is an effective way to mount an offensive against your opponent, the Deep Throat Corollary proves that the same can be true when rebutting someone else's attack.

In 1992, the Wayne Owens campaign attempted to remind voters of his opponent Bob Bennett's ties to Washington, primarily through his connections to the Watergate scandal two decades before.[39] In 1992, speculation still swirled around the identity of Deep Throat, the scandal's chief informant to *Washington Post* reporters Bob Woodward and Carl Bernstein. Bennett had close ties to important players in the event and was suspected by some to be the anonymous Deep Throat.

Bennett owned a public relations firm that functioned as a front for the Central Intelligence Agency. One of his employees, Howard Hunt, organized the Watergate break-in. Bennett had an established relationship with Woodward, and he previously held a prominent position with the Nixon Administration. The former president himself allegedly suggested that Bennett could be the unknown informant. Only years later would Deep Throat's true identity be unveiled as former FBI agent Mark Felt.

The prospect of Watergate attacks in the 1992 race clearly unsettled the Bennett campaign from the very beginning. Bennett shared a letter sent from Howard Baker, former senator and ranking member of the U.S

---

[39] In a little known Utah connection to the Watergate scandal, Church of Jesus Christ of Latter-day Saints Apostle D. Todd Christofferson was a law clerk for John J. Sirica, the judge who ordered Nixon to turn over the controversial White House tapes. Christofferson would be one of the very first people to ever listen to the secret tapes. On the Nixon Presidential Library's official website, I recently tried to pull up the 1973 oral history interview of Elder Christofferson. When I clicked on it to listen to the recording, the webpage says that the audio file can no longer be found. I'm doing my best to not read too much into this.

Senate Watergate Committee, exonerating him of any involvement in the affair. But even that didn't seem to shake the issue with the local media.[40]

The successful rebuttal to the argument came from Owens himself. During a radio interview some time before the campaign had fully begun, a reporter asked Owens what he thought about Bennett's involvement in the Watergate scandal. Owens responded, "No, I don't think Bob Bennett played a major role in Watergate." Months later when these allegations resurfaced and gained traction among voters, Bennett created a commercial where he refuted the claims of involvement in Watergate. At the end of the commercial, he pressed play on a tape recorder that repeated his opponent's words three times, "No I don't think Bob Bennett played a major role in Watergate."

The issue lifted and Bennett went on to easily defeat Owens. If you're going to refute your opponent's attack, always remember that using their own words can be your most powerful defense.

---

[40] Another Utah connection to the Watergate affair was a BYU student hired to spy on the Democratic campaign on behalf of the Nixon campaign. Not only did he give information to Nixon loyalist Howard Hunt each week at a D.C. drugstore on the corner of 17th and K Street NW (add this site to your D.C. travel itinerary), he also provided Hunt a floor plan of the McGovern headquarters and shepherded one of the Watergate burglars through the office where he unsuccessfully attempted to plant an eavesdropping device.*
*Walter Rugaber, "Watergate Trial Hears Hunt Offer to Plead Guilty." *New York Times*, 11 January 1973.

GETTING "CHAFFETZED"

Loyalty is hard to come by in politics.

In a tweet about Congressman Jason Chaffetz's last-minute decision to challenge House Majority Leader Kevin McCarthy, former Utah Governor Jon Huntsman conveyed his disappointment in the decision on social media by tweeting, "@GOPLeaderMcCarthy just got 'Chaffetzed.' Something I know a little something about. #selfpromoter #powerhungry"

Chaffetz had previously served as the chief of staff to Huntsman before eventually turning against his former boss in his 2012 presidential campaign.[41] Loyalty is often difficult to come by in politics, something Huntsman learned with his former friend.

When Governor Norm Bangerter faced a stiff Republican challenge during his 1988 reelection, he commented publicly about his former supporter-turned-opponent, "There are no friendships in politics. There are just coalitions, and I guess our coalition is over."[42]

There is perhaps no greater blow to a candidate than when a former friend turns against them. While it is admittedly rare, it can be devastating in the moment. There is nothing more valuable (or scarce) in politics than loyalty.

---

[41] In Chaffetz's defense, Huntsman had fired him as his chief of staff. One *Deseret News* article reported, "A member of the staff walked into the governor's office and delivered some unsettling news: if Huntsman didn't fire Chaffetz, the rest of the staff would quit." Jesse Hyde and Eric Schulzke, "The calculus behind Jason Chaffetz's sudden decision to walk away." *Deseret News*, 21 April 2017.

[42] This opponent to Governor Bangerter was ironically Jon Huntsman Sr.

THE BOUNTIFUL PRECINCT 12 RULE

Never underestimate the value of psychological warfare.

During his run for an unprecedented seventh term, U.S. Senator Orrin Hatch received his most vigorous challenge in the Republican primary. After his colleague U.S. Senator Bob Bennett was defeated at the 2010 Republican convention, many political observers believed Hatch would likely suffer a similar fate.

On caucus night when delegates to the GOP state convention would be elected, Hatch executed a brilliant statewide strategy to elect pro-Hatch supporters. However, this wasn't enough for one of the state's shrewdest campaigners, Orrin Hatch.

He decided to run up the score. In the home precinct of his main challenger Dan Liljenquist (Bountiful Precinct 12), the Hatch campaign pushed to win every delegate slot to embarrass his opponent in his own neighborhood. Of course he also made sure to do everything he could to encourage reporters to be there to see the carnage firsthand.

The extra effort just to win a few delegates did not matter much in the overall campaign, but it did play with the psyche of his opponent's campaign.[43] It also built a media narrative that was difficult to overcome for his ultimately unsuccessful challenger.

---

[43] Statewide campaigns frequently send a staffer to follow around and videotape an opponent. The explanation is that they want video of any potential campaign blunder (think "Macaca"), but the biggest benefit is the psychological toll it takes on your opponent.

THE HOLE N" THE ROCK RULE

Avoid basic grammar and spelling mistakes.[44]

If you're ever visiting southeastern Utah, about 12 miles south of Moab, you have likely come across the strange 5,000 square-foot store and museum carved into the side of the sandstone.[45] Above the store in huge white letters is painted the words, Hole N" the Rock.

The stray quotation mark is confusing for any copy editor who might be visiting the area. An apostrophe before the "N" could have worked, but a quotation mark after it leaves everyone confused.[46]

Campaigns have endured endless ridicule for poor spelling and with good reason.[47] Look at every campaign mailer or flyer you send out as if it were a professional résumé. Even one small spelling error can be glaring in such an important piece.

---

[44] Please reference this rule when you inevitably find errors in this book.

[45] Not to be confused with the gas station in Hanksville that is carved into the side of the rock. Or that one strange Bed and Breakfast in southeastern Utah where a polygamist family once lived.

[46] Honorable mention for naming rights to the Hole N" The Rock Rule also went to the BYU Daily Universe April 6, 2009 edition for printing a caption to a photo of LDS leaders as members of the "Quorum of Twelve Apostates." Prominent Washington journalist McKay Coppins was the editor of the paper at the time but had no role in the mistake. The other honorable mention was a 1998 *Herald Journal* ad for the Cache Valley Mall that was ridiculed on the *David Letterman Show*. It was a Christmas ad that mistakenly spelled the word Santa, instead saying in prominent letters, "Hey kids, grab your parents and come to the Cache Valley Mall for Satan's arrival."

[47] You say "potato," Dan Quayle says "potatoe."

THE BUCKSHOT THEORY

Some Utahns love a good conspiracy theory.

During the lead up to the 2018 Republican state convention, delegates received a barrage of communications from various party insiders about an alleged plot undertaken by a secret cabal of establishment Republicans seeking to destroy the party's caucus-convention system. The focus of their ire was the Buckshot Caucus, a small Facebook group organized by longtime party activists Jeremy Roberts and Carl Downing.

The group's online description reads, "Like the Illuminati...but with bacon...and guns." In a *Salt Lake Tribune* investigative article on the alleged conspiracy, a prominent state senator referred to the group's name as an inside joke of people who like, "guns, Diet Coke and bacon."

Yet the conspiracy theories continued to fly throughout the 2018 cycle, including campaign signs at the state convention warning delegates of the group. To anyone on the outside, the issue seemed confusing if not laughable.

The more ideologically extreme an individual is, the more susceptible they become to conspiracy theories.[48] This is especially true of delegates to the state's respective political conventions.[49]

---

[48] One of Utah's most brilliant campaign strategists, David Jacobs, owns a consulting firm called The Grassy Knoll LLC.
[49] I participate on a podcast with a regular segment called "Conspiracy Corner." The introduction is always, "Brought to you by the help desk of the Republican state convention."

THE EAGLE SCOUT RULE

Certain references in your political biography undermine your credibility.

A candidate's campaign website will often present a personal biography of a candidate's background to help humanize the candidate. But if your personal biography mentions your Eagle Scout award, then I'm guessing you're probably not a very viable candidate.[50]

To give you a feel for some issues to be avoided in a candidate biography, here are just a few examples from the 2018 U.S. Senate race:[51]

Candidate A:
"In high school he was a member of USA Table Tennis, and also competed in the Westinghouse Science Talent Search and the National Junior Science and Humanities Symposium based on his high school research with wheat germ DNA."

Candidate B:
"She is a published author of medieval fiction and enjoys riding her horse and hiking with the family dogs."

Candidate C:
"He enjoys starting his days with long walks and weight lifting. He ends his days with dinner and reading scriptures with his family."

Candidate D:
"I am not a politician, nor do I want to be. I am a working-class father,

---

[50] Now if you were a Silver Buffalo, that's a completely different story.

[51] One of the candidates in this race went by the name, "Abe Lincoln Brian Jenkins" See the Abe Lincoln Jenkins Rule (p. 162). And yes, he dressed up as Honest Abe. His website said the following: "In addition to his passion for freedom, he's also an actor and a speaker. And so he brings something unique as a Lincoln impersonator....And to the delight of many audiences, he is a near exact replica of Abraham Lincoln. That is, he is quite possibly the most look-alike Lincoln on the planet today."

husband, brother and neighbor who has experienced medical bankruptcy, unemployment, tax debt and disillusionment with government, who is also committed to making a difference."

Candidate E:
"My Major Political Influences: George Washington, John Adams, Thomas Jefferson, James Madison, Alexander Hamilton, Calvin Coolidge, Phyllis Schlafly, Milton Friedman, Ronald Reagan, 1990s-era Rush Limbaugh,[52] Ron Paul, Dennis Prager, Mark Levin, and Ben Shapiro."

Those were all from candidate websites for the same political office. Without knowing anything else about them, many voters immediately eliminate them from consideration based on just a few small facts.

Stick to the basics in your personal biography. Avoid embellishment or obscure references that aren't related to the office.

---

[52] I've spent a significant amount of time analyzing why the candidate felt the need to distinguish 1990s Rush Limbaugh from present-day Rush Limbaugh. I have theories if you'd like to talk about it.

THE CONDOLEEZZA RICE ENDORSEMENT

Prominent endorsements from national Republicans are seldom helpful.

During the vicious 2012 election between Democrat Jim Matheson and his Republican challenger Mia Love, prominent leaders from across the country came to the state to offer their endorsement to the Love campaign. One of these events was headlined by former Secretary of State Condoleezza Rice.

Matheson blasted the endorsements, telling the *Salt Lake Tribune,* "Condi Rice doesn't know my opponent and she doesn't know me and she doesn't know Utah."[53]

Even Republican Congressman Rob Bishop agreed with his Democratic colleague's take, "The bottom line is, these type of people coming in add some kind of focus to [the campaign] but sometimes they're also distracting...The bottom line is she's still running a Utah race about Utah issues and Utah concerns."[54]

While the allure of a big name may seem appealing in your race, they frequently offer little benefit and may backfire. They may draw attention to your candidacy in the news cycle for that day, but it can also distract from the larger message your campaign is hoping to drive.[55]

Often the distraction just isn't worth it.

---

[53] Robert Gehrke, "During Utah fundraiser, Rice warns of 'entitlement mentality." *Salt Lake Tribune,* 10 September 2012.

[54] Robert Gehrke, "Boehner raises money for Love, says nation can't weather more Obama." *Salt Lake Tribune,* 16 August 2012.

[55] See the Natalie Gochnour Rule (p. 51).

THE WARREN HATCH COROLLARY

Occasionally a national endorsement can make the difference in an election.

During the closing days of the 1976 Republican primary election between frontrunner Jack Carlson and newcomer Orrin Hatch, the Hatch campaign made a last-minute effort to garner the endorsement of California Governor and failed presidential candidate, Ronald Reagan.[56]

The Reagan camp sent the Hatch campaign a telegram announcing their support with one small problem. Instead of announcing his endorsement of "Orrin" Hatch, the telegram from Governor Reagan expressed his support for "Warren" Hatch.[57] Working quickly, the Hatch campaign modified the typo in the telegram and pushed out the announcement to the local media.

Trailing in polling during the final days leading up to the election, Hatch easily defeated his Republican opponent who credited his victory to the last-minute endorsement by the popular Reagan.

By and large, national leaders seldom help in your campaign, but every once in a while it can make the difference.

---

[56] At the time of the endorsement, Reagan had just been defeated for the GOP presidential nomination by President Gerald Ford.

[57] As a history teacher at Snow College, I required my students to pass the U.S. Citizenship Exam. One question is, "Who is one of your state's U.S. Senators now?" My all-time favorite response from a student was, "Orrin Jeffs."

THE BANGERTER ENDORSEMENT

An endorsement from a prominent Utah politician can give legitimacy to an upstart's campaign.

When Mike Lee decided to challenge incumbent U.S. Senator Bob Bennett, very few people felt like he had much of a chance. Even Lee's eventual GOP primary opponent, Tim Bridgewater, began campaigning for the GOP state chair position before pivoting to the U.S. Senate race.[58]

Lee's political fate changed the day former Governor Norm Bangerter and Congressman Jim Hansen announced in a press conference that they were endorsing the young politician. While most endorsements offer minimal value to the candidate, the Bangerter support immediately gave legitimacy to the challenger Lee's campaign.

If you are challenging an established incumbent,[59] you don't need more endorsements than they have, you just need somebody. Governor Bangerter and Congressman Hansen gave the Lee campaign immediate legitimacy as he made his case to Utah voters.

---

[58] Both Bridgewater and Lee proved that getting into a race early is not always the best course of action, contrary to popular belief.

[59] If you plan to challenge an incumbent, I would encourage you to study the military strategies associated with asymmetrical warfare. If George Washington had attacked the British head on, we would have lost the Revolutionary War. Insurgent political campaigns could learn a thing or two from such conflicts. Getting your opponent to debate* you isn't a strategy. You can be more creative than that.

* On the note of debates, my personal favorite moderator is the brilliant David Magleby, a longtime professor of political science at BYU.

THE KIRKHAM ENDORSMENT

Receiving an opponent's endorsement can be extremely valuable.

This rule obviously applies to intra-party fights in either party conventions or primaries. It derives its name from business executive and Tea Party leader David Kirkham, who ran unsuccessfully for governor against incumbent Republican Gary Herbert.

After being eliminated in an earlier round of voting, Kirkham announced his support of Herbert to the surprise of delegates in attendance, helping the governor earn 63 percent of the vote to avoid a primary. Herbert's main challenger credited the Kirkham endorsement with pushing the governor over the 60 percent threshold in the race to win outright.

The spontaneous nature of political conventions make candidate endorsements especially valuable for potential candidates.[60] The convention hall can appear in disarray, as delegates who supported eliminated candidates try to decide who to vote for next.

In such an atmosphere, a cue from their preferred candidate can often move some delegates towards a specific candidate.

---

[60] The politics of endorsements can also be very bitter between the respective campaigns. In a 2012 congressional race, defeated candidate Carl Wimmer accused his fellow challenger Stephen Sandstrom of having "sold his soul" when he chose to back a different candidate.

THE MITT NON-ENDORSEMENT ENDORSEMENT

Some candidates will imply an endorsement, even if they never received one.

This rule derives its name from the numerous Utah politicians who posted on campaign websites and brochures pictures of themselves with 2012 Republican presidential nominee Mitt Romney. While they technically never said that Romney was endorsing their candidacy, the picture left no doubt in the minds of voters.

This strategy can be risky, as the supposed endorser may be offended by the action and potential turn toward your opponent in intra-party primaries. While such a response would hardly ever occur, it is always best to stick to the facts. If someone is unwilling to give you their endorsement, then you shouldn't pretend to have received it.

THE FRANK LAYDEN RULE

Humor can be used to relieve political tension.

In Utah sports, Frank Layden was the perfect deliverer of a punchline. At the Delta Center dedication, he spoke of his own experience coming to Utah. "You know, eleven years ago I walked into this valley and said, 'This is definitely not the place.' Well I was wrong."

When he was criticized for his decision to trade Dominique Wilkins, he joked, "What? I thought I was trading Jeff Wilkins."

Layden's quick wit helped diffuse the tension of those first years of a struggling Jazz franchise. Lacking stars in their new Utah home and with one of the league's lowest payrolls, Layden somehow managed to keep the Jazz relevant during those early years. For a team without much of a history or identity, it was Layden and his constant humor that formed the foundation. In many ways, without him we could have very easily lost the team to another city.

In politics, you will face many angry constituents and difficult debates. Keeping a sense of humor helps to level off the stress of such difficult times. A well-timed joke or funny story can help smooth the edges off any unpleasant interaction. Layden always used self-deprecation so as not to be offensive. Follow a similar pattern to discover new ways to ease tension and continue fighting for another day.[61]

---

[61] Watching Layden handle the transition to his successor Jerry Sloan is also instructive. He never undermined Sloan or second guessed the coach. At times, it can be difficult to watch someone sit in the same seat you used to hold, but critiquing their service is considered poor form.

THE SHARLENE WELLS THEORY

After a scandal, the most clean-cut candidate often wins.

Following controversy in the 1984 Miss America Pageant, Utahn Sharlene Wells won the 1985 award in what many viewed as a path to overcoming the organization's recent experience with scandal. The previous year's winner had been forced to give up her title when nude photographs had been published of her in a national magazine. By contrast, the clean-cut Utahn went on to be an outspoken supporter of conservative issues while representing the organization.

Similarly, when a scandal surprisingly took down Bob Livingston, the heir apparent to become U.S. Speaker of the House after the 1998 elections, House Republicans turned to Dennis Hastert, a non-controversial representative from Illinois with a low public profile.[62]

Don't be surprised if the mold for success suddenly changes thanks to a scandal. Rather than change yourself, embracing your own differences can be what leads you to future political success. In general, politics is an unpredictable enterprise. What holds you back today may be the very thing that propels you forward tomorrow.

---

[62] Hastert would later be embroiled in a scandal far worse than Livingston's.

THE OKERLUND THEORY

Be aggressive when rebutting an unfair attack.

Because Utahns are so agreeable, many people falsely claim that negative attacks don't work in the Beehive State. Nothing could be further from the truth. The lesson of Utah Senator Ralph Okerlund[63] is instructive on how best to handle this situation.

During a 2012 Utah Senate election, Okerlund's opponent began attacking the Senator on a variety of issues. A former dairy farmer, Okerlund immediately sent out mailers calling "bull" on his opponent for the blatant mischaracterization of his positions. The speed and aggressiveness with which Okerlund responded worked to immediately turn voters away from the attacks.[64]

As Utahns, we hate negativity. However, when someone else is negative, you can absolutely attack their negative message while still taking the high road. In other words, negative attacks don't work unless you're rebutting a perceived attack. The key is to not throw the first punch.

While Utah's culture can be passive aggressive, it is important to point out this is not always the case. Utahns have a strong sense of fair play, and any candidate violates this at their own peril.[65]

---

[63] Governor Mike Leavitt's middle name is Okerlund, along with each of his five younger brothers in honor of his mother's maiden name.

[64] Assisting Okerlund in the race was political wunderkind Casey Hill.

[65] There was no one better than Congressman Jim Matheson at getting Utahns to call an opponent's attack out of bounds without incurring the same damage to his own campaign.

THE MATHESON = PELOSI RULE

Simplicity is best.

One of the most successful campaign messages was delivered during the 2010 2nd District race between incumbent Jim Matheson and his Republican challenger Morgan Philpot. As the campaign heated up, lawn signed popped up throughout the state saying only, "Matheson = Pelosi."

The message was simple. A vote for the Democrat Matheson would lead to a likely Speaker of the House Nancy Pelosi. Ultimately Matheson prevailed in the race, but Philpot outperformed expectations in the close contest.[66]

When running for office, too many campaigns get lost in a host of issues that distract from the campaign's central message. If you choose to put up a billboard, keep the sign to less than six total words,[67] including your name and logo.[68] When writing a letter, focus on a few key bullet points.

Boil down the argument for your candidacy to as simple a message as possible. A disciplined candidate is frequently a successful candidate.

---

[66] Some candidates have subsequently tried to adopt the exact same campaign tactic. As always, just because something worked years before for someone else doesn't mean copying it will work for you too.

[67] The six-word limit is also a good rule of thumb for applause lines in a speech.

[68] That rule came from U.S. Senator Bob Bennett. Any time a staff member drove him around the state, he loved to critique billboards. His playful 2004 campaign billboards were especially successful, including the following phrases:

- Bold. Brilliant. Beanpole.
- Big heart. Big ideas. Big ears.
- Able. Articulate. Aerodynamic.
- Honest. Humble. Hairless.
- Better looking than Abraham Lincoln (Barely).

THE SUPER DELL 2.6 PERCENT RULE

Votes are often cast in protest, not in support of any particular candidate.

In his 2008 run for Utah governor,[69] Dell "SUPERDELL" Schanze had some interesting policy proposals. In one ad attacking Governor Jon Huntsman Jr., Schanze said the following: "[Super Dell]: All of our cars will run on water. I know. My friend has run his 4-stroke weed eater completely on water. The technology is real and has been suppressed by socialists like Huntsman."

Huntsman wasn't the only one to receive Super Dell's ire. The well-known Utah celebrity criticized the media when his company, "Totally Awesome Computers" closed saying, "It's too bad that all of the media in Utah are liars and murderers. You just destroyed the greatest computer company of all time. We were the best in the world, the world champion. All this hatred was created by you. You're basically angels of Satan."

And yet despite all of that, Super Dell still managed to receive 24,820 votes, 2.6 percent of all votes cast.[70] Could you really find enough people to fill up the Delta Center[71] who are passionate Super Dell supporters?[72] It turns out, people like to cast a protest vote. This number will inevitably rise if the race is considered uncompetitive.

---

[69] Super Dell's runs for governor (he also ran for governor in 2010) were actually not his first campaigns for public office. He first ran for mayor of Saratoga Springs against Mia Love. She was a member of the city council at the time, and the race generated little publicity. Except that in true Super Dell fashion, he got detained by police on Election Day for breaking the law and campaigning in a polling place.
[70] I was really hoping this number was 0.05 or 3.2 percent for the inevitable DABC jokes.
[71] I will forever refer to the Utah Jazz arena as the Delta Center.
[72] When I ran for county commission years ago, one of my opponents said, "When I ran for Congress, I had enough people who voted for me to fill up the LDS Conference Center." It sounds impressive on its face, but then you realize it's a backward way of saying you only received 2.6 percent of the vote. This same opponent gave a speech at our county convention, where he concluded his remarks by saying, "Just remember, only one of us up here is one call away from Mitt Romney." To this day, I am still confused (and curious) by what he meant.

THE UTE PAC COROLLARY

Third party candidates can be a spoiler.

While it is almost unheard of for a third party candidate to win a Utah race,[73] the Super Dell 2.6 Percent Rule can be used in competitive elections to benefit one of the two major candidates. Republicans would like a Green Party member to run, and Democrats would prefer a Libertarian or Independent American candidate to draw away votes from their opponent.

Political action committees have learned the importance of this issue over the years, and in 2012 the Democratic UTE PAC spent approximately $10,000 in voter outreach efforts to Republicans, making the argument that Libertarian candidate Jim Vein was the best choice in the increasingly acrimonious race between incumbent Jim Matheson and his Republican challenger Mia Love.

In the end, Love was defeated by a meager 768 votes. Of note, Libertarian candidate Jim Vein received 6,400 votes (not coincidentally 2.6 percent of the total vote). If Vein had not run, it is likely that Love would have defeated Matheson in the race.

---

[73] Likely the biggest exception to this was in the early 1900s, when a number of Socialist Party candidates were elected to local offices. In all, more than 100 Socialists were elected in cities including Salt Lake City, Cedar City, Murray, Eureka, Fillmore, Monroe, Salina, Bingham and other communities. According to longtime Utah historian John R. Sillito, Utah was also one of only 18 states in the nation that elected a member of the Socialist Party to its legislature (J. Alex Bevan from Tooele County in 1915). To learn more, check out Sillito's book, *History of Utah Radicalism: Startling, Socialistic, and Decidedly Revolutionary.*

THE JUDICIAL RETENTION COROLLARY

Even the most extreme candidates will start with some base of support.

Despite the number of judicial retention choices on the ballot, almost all of them receive a strikingly similar number of votes.[74] The lack of disparity in almost every race leads to the logical conclusion that Utahns are not analyzing judges one-by-one but rather voting to retain them all or get rid of them all.[75]

This information is valuable in determining the base of support for a challenger to an incumbent, particularly in a primary election when party affiliation is not an issue.

My floor for a challenger to an incumbent is the average number of Utahns who vote no on a judicial retention race. In most years, that number ranges between 18-25 percent of the total vote. Utahns who vote no on all judges are also likely to vote against all incumbents. Therefore, a challenger can reasonably expect to start a race with at least that much support.[76] When a candidate fails to achieve even 30 percent of the vote in a primary election in a two-way race, it is a sign that the candidate has virtually no support among the general public beyond the "Just Say No" base of support.

---

[74] While Utah voters have never removed a Supreme Court justice, there have been a small number of lower court judges who have been removed via the retention vote.

[75] Why we have straight-ticket voting in Utah but no mechanism to "Retain All" or "Not Retain All" judges is a mystery to me.

[76] The calculation is admittedly imprecise as judicial retention elections only occur during a general election cycle.

THE JACK CARLSON RULE

Leaders of the pack will try to ignore their lesser-known opponents.

Most Utah politicos remember the 2012 U.S. Senate election when challenger Dan Liljenquist repeatedly challenged U.S. Senator Orrin Hatch to debates. In each case, Hatch either declined the invitation or ignored it altogether. It got to the point that Liljenquist even debated a cardboard cutout of Hatch to prove his point.

Interestingly, when Hatch first ran for U.S. Senate in 1976, he experienced the very same problem against the frontrunner in that race, Jack Carlson. In his autobiography, Hatch recorded the following about that 1976 race: "I desperately tried to get [Carlson] to debate, knowing, as the underdog and lesser-known candidate, that a debate could only raise my profile. He constantly refused, choosing instead to emphasize that I had lived in Utah for only six years."[77]

As a challenger, you will need to find other ways to get your campaign message out. Without fail, campaign frontrunners will try to ignore their struggling opponents.

---

[77] Hatch's book *Square Peg: Confessions of a Citizen Senator* was actually a fun read, especially the section where he shows a significant amount of self-awareness in discussing his failed presidential run. Hatch also states that when President Clinton had an opening to appoint a Supreme Court justice, it was the Utah Senator who first suggested he nominate Ruth Bader Ginsburg, a candidate the president had not previously considered. In other words, there is no Notorious RBG without first the Notorious OGH.*

*This footnote is brought to you by the critically-acclaimed book, *The Exorcist*.

THE ROB BISHOP TOASTMASTERS CLUB

Politicians are surprisingly poor at giving speeches.

You would think that someone who spends so much time giving speeches would be better at it, but many Utah politicians continue to struggle with the simple, yet nuanced skill. If you have attended a county or state political convention, you know what I mean.

That is until Congressman Rob Bishop takes the stage and immediately has the audience hanging on his every word. I am only half joking with the Toastmasters Club reference. I really think Utah politicians could learn a lot from Brigham City's favorite son.[78]

Keys to Rob Bishop's success are his quick delivery and memorable one-liners. Too often politicians give either a confusing or overly memorized delivery that fails to land with listeners. Others are entirely predictable, giving the same speech over and over again.[79]

Next time you have to give a speech, listen to Rob Bishop. We all could learn a lot.

---

[78] A close second to Bishop's impressive speech delivery is Michelle Quist, an accomplished attorney and former Secretary of the Utah Republican Party.
[79] The joke among candidates making the county convention circuit is that candidates could just as easily give their opponent's speech because they've heard it so many times.

THE REED BULLEN RULE

Speeches can never be too short.

Before the governor's annual State of the State speech was broadcast on local television, Utah Governor Cal Rampton once delivered a two-hour State of the State address to the Legislature with a short recess included. At the conclusion of his remarks, Senate President (and prominent LDS church leader) Reed Bullen[80] jokingly commented, "I think, governor, that's the longest speech I ever listened to." Rampton responded by saying, "I'll have to watch that, Reed, because when a Mormon stake president complains about the length of a speech, there's certainly room for concern."[81]

Politicians frequently forget this important rule. They drag on, discussing issues that are of little import to those listening. While any good politician must have a deep understanding of the policies they are promoting, you don't need to prove that deep understanding in every one of your day-to-day interactions.

When in doubt, keep it short. And above all, always leave your audience wanting more.

---

[80] Bullen was one of Utah's true visionaries. Together with his father and son, he would pioneer numerous advances in media from their rural Cache Valley home. The family was central to the efforts to bring newspapers, radio and cable television to northern Utah. They also have been longtime supporters of Aggie athletics so you know they must be good people.
[81] Calvin L. Rampton, Floyd A. O'Neil, and Gregory C. Thompson, *As I Recall* (Salt Lake City: University of Utah Press, 1989), 134.

THE TIM BRIDGEWATER RULE

After defeating an opponent, always be gracious.

Tim Bridgewater has always been brilliant in Utah state GOP conventions. One of Utah's most impressive politicians, Bridgewater was narrowly defeated in his congressional and Senate bids. But each time, he exceeded expectations at state conventions.

While this success can be attributed to a host of factors, one area where Bridgewater far outshined most politicians was his second and third round convention speeches. Candidates frequently practice their first speeches ad nauseam, but they often shoot from the hip in subsequent rounds.[82] This is perhaps understandable, since a second speech is never a guarantee and its time is almost always limited to only one or two minutes.

Whether or not Bridgewater practiced the speech, he was a master at delivering it. He always devoted the overwhelming majority of his limited time to thanking the candidates who had just been eliminated. He mentioned them by name and asked the crowd of delegates to join him in applauding them.

During the first round of balloting in the 2010 U.S. Senate race, Bridgewater trailed Mike Lee by two percent. After the second round of voting, Bridgewater led Lee by 1.5 percent. After the third and final round, Bridgewater led by nearly 15 percent and narrowly missed reaching the 60-percent threshold to avoid a primary election.

This model of convention speeches is remarkably effective, especially when other candidates are not devoting time in a similar fashion. The simple technique shows the candidate to be a gracious winner, and don't

---

[82] Resist the urge to invite all of your supporters on stage with you during your speech. The awkward and time-consuming walk up on stage is ineffective.

forget, the remaining delegates deciding who to vote for were supporters of those defeated opponents. In comparison, his final opponent made his closing argument by showing a video from U.S. Senator Jim DeMint in lieu of a candidate speech.[83] Very few in the room knew DeMint, likely intended to have more of an impact against an expected final round matchup with the incumbent U.S. Senator rather than the outsider Bridgewater.

Remember the Tim Bridgewater Rule if you are ever tempted to spike the ball in your moment of temporary victory.[84] Always be gracious to your opponents, especially those you have just defeated. Voters appreciate a helping hand up to those who have been so publicly humbled.

---

[83] Never show a video at a convention. Bridgewater technically broke this rule when he showed a video to introduce his first convention speech in the 2010 race. I forgive this error because in the clip he had excellent form when throwing a football.

[84] Bridgewater had one of the most distinguishable voices in Utah political history. Described at times as either gravelly or raspy, he frequently poked fun at his own voice but it never seemed to harm him in his various political runs.

A MILT HANKS MOMENT

Political conventions can swing on the smallest of factors.

During the 2012 Republican convention, 11 Republican candidates vied to win the party's nomination at the state GOP's nominating convention. As is often the case in political conventions, some candidates were more serious than others. Most political observers believed that former Speaker of the House David Clark was the frontrunner, but a primary election was likely.

One candidate that everyone agreed didn't stand a chance was Eureka Mayor Milt Hanks. Lacking the campaign infrastructure to mount a serious campaign, most expected Hanks to drop off the ballot in the first round with only a handful of votes.

He was assigned the last speaking slot right before delegates went to vote and when his time arrived immediately launched into a conspiracy-ridden accusation against four of his fellow candidates. He alleged that they had worked together to unfairly target another candidate, Chris Stewart, through a mystery letter that no one had seen.[85]

"Are we back to the hog trough of backroom deals and backstabbing politics?" Hanks asked delegates in his speech. "It's the same stuff I shoveled off the floor of the chicken coop."[86]

With the accusations dropping just minutes before delegates would vote, the other candidates had no opportunity to respond. As initial votes were tallied, Stewart immediately jumped to the lead.

---

[85] The letter alleged that Stewart had a role in the infamous "Temple Mailer" from the 2010 election which was crafted by his brother, Tim Stewart, a former Bob Bennett aide.
[86] On the subject of chicken coops, U.S. Senator Orrin Hatch loved to tell the story of him fixing up an old chicken coop that he lived in with his wife while he attended law school at the University of Pittsburgh.

From there the convention hall turned into mass hysteria.

One of the accused candidates took to the microphone and attacked Stewart for being a "bald-faced liar." Multiple candidates had their microphones cut for attacks on others. Several withdrew their candidacy and threw their support to Clark. Other candidates suggested that Hanks was a plant from the Stewart campaign.

Stewart emerged victorious with 60 percent of the vote and avoided a primary. Subsequent to the election, four candidates accused Stewart of election fraud in a Federal Elections Commission complaint.[87]

In many ways, the Milt Hanks Moment is similar to what other campaigns refer to as an October Surprise, a last minute attack that other candidates cannot respond to in adequate time. The difference is that these attacks are much more effective in a convention setting.

It's really a matter of math. The smaller a pool of voters, the more likely last-minute attacks can work. Historically, Utah political conventions have been dominated by a relatively small pool of delegates with the outcome of a race often determined by only a handful of people.

As a result, political conventions are wildly unpredictable in comparison to more traditional primary and general elections. Whether it's a Temple Mailer or some other last-minute attack, voters can quickly change their minds and dramatically alter the outcome of a race.

Expect a political convention to be unpredictable to even the most astute political insiders.

---

[87] No action was ever taken by the FEC against Stewart.

THE JOE CANNON RULE

A one-party dominant state will have more divisions within the dominant party.

Someone once complained to former Utah Republican Chairman Joe Cannon about Utah being a one-party state.[88] He quickly replied, "We're a three-party state, and I preside over two of them."[89]

With Utah's overwhelming Republican majority comes more division within the same Republican Party. GOP supporters know that only in the most extreme situations could the Republican candidate be defeated in the general election, and consequently internal divisions frequently emerge.

In many ways, we have seen this issue play out in the internal Republican debate on the future of the caucus-convention system. While each side makes arguments about the value of each system, what it really comes down to is who controls the party. Until the Democratic Party serves as a sufficient check on the GOP, these internal divisions will continue to exist.

---

[88] My first political memory occurred during Joe Cannon's 1992 U.S. Senate race. I was only eight years old at the time, but I distinctly remember him coming to the Sanpete County Fair in his natural-gas vehicle.

[89] Robert Bennett, "More political participation needed." *Deseret News*, 15 December 2014.

THE CHASE PETERSON RULE

People in entry-level positions on a campaign often have the most insight.

University of Utah Athletic Director Chris Hill should be given credit for the tremendous hire of Utah legend Rick Majerus. However, before he could move forward with the hiring, University of Utah President[90] Chase Peterson decided to do something a little unorthodox. Peterson found a player from Majerus's previous team who had been a starter his junior year before riding the bench for almost the entirety of his senior season.

Peterson asked the player what he thought of Majerus as a coach. According to Peterson, the player said, "Next to my father, Coach Majerus is the most important man in my life."[91]

With that response, Majerus had the job and the University of Utah's basketball team went on to have phenomenal success.[92]

Similarly, in politics you can learn a lot about someone's campaign from the frontline volunteers or employees. A successful campaign will have a vibrancy to it that can be felt from top to bottom.

Note to potential candidates: check in with your grassroots team regularly. They will have far more insight into your campaign than high-paid consultants. One of the greatest dangers to any candidate is isolation, cutting off valuable information to the candidate. Do not simply rely on others for the latest intel. Get out there and learn for yourself.

---

[90] If you ever attend a meeting at the University of Utah presidential home, take a minute to contemplate the influence of two of Utah's finest community leaders, Joseph and Evelyn Rosenblatt, who donated the home (their former residence) to the university. An entire book deserves to be written about these incredible Utah business and community icons.
[91] Rick Majerus, *My Life on a Napkin: Pillow Mints, Playground Dreams, and Coaching the Runnin Utes.* (New York: Hyperion, 2000), 54.
[92] The Utah Legislature just began an audit of that last sentence.

THE SANDBAGGING STATE STREET PRINCIPLE

Utahns are anxious to volunteer for a worthy cause.

On Memorial Day weekend in 1983, City Creek spilled over its banks and rushed into Salt Lake City's downtown district. As the flooding overwhelmed city crews, thousands of volunteers joined in the rescue effort and helped turn one of Salt Lake City's most trafficked streets into a sandbagged river. Crews replicated the same technique on several other city streets, prompting one newspaper to proudly call Salt Lake City, "the Venice of the high desert."[93]

Across the country, community volunteerism has declined dramatically. However, one state continues to excel in this area, as year after year Utah tops national rankings. Over that one 1983 weekend, volunteers filled and placed more sandbags than the entire population of Salt Lake City. Media accounts from across the country heralded the city's volunteer efforts with constant praise. This prompted Salt Lake City Mayor Ted Wilson to proudly state that the effort of local volunteers was "comparable to building the great pyramid in 30 hours."[94] The Salt Lake National Weather Service ranked the 1983 floods as the most significant weather event of the past century in the state. And yet, the memory most Utahns have of it is not the damage that occurred, but rather the spirit of volunteerism that permeated the community.

In every political campaign, there is a need for volunteers. Campaigns often struggle to recruit volunteers despite Utah's unparalleled leadership on this issue.[95] Help your supporters find value in their service, and they will be much more likely to assist in your time of need.

---

[93] Jay Mathews, "Salt Lake City Keeps Its Oars in the Water, Eyes on the Weather." *Washington Post*, 7 June 1983.

[94] "Creek flooding takes holiday – a change from weekend of sandbagging 3 years ago." *Deseret News*, 26 May 1986.

[95] The one major exception to this being the legendary George Zinn who has volunteered so often he is affectionately referred to by insiders as one of the Three Nephites.

THE BANGERTER COMEBACK

Never give up hope in your campaign.

No Utah incumbent has ever overcome steeper odds than former Utah Governor Norm Bangerter's 1988 election. Mired in a deep recession, Bangerter had recently overseen the largest tax increase in Utah history. Anti-tax protesters led a statewide referendum opposing the increases, further harming Bangerter's reelection prospects.

Popular Salt Lake City Mayor Ted Wilson began the race with a commanding 35-percent lead. Former Republican Merrill Cook announced he would challenge Bangerter as an independent, bleeding away Republican votes from the incumbent. And perhaps in the worst days of the Bangerter campaign, successful businessman Jon Huntsman Sr. announced that he would challenge the governor for the Republican nomination. Prominent Utah Republicans publicly begged Bangerter to drop out of the race for the good of the party.[96] Most candidates would have given up at this point in time to try and save face, but not Bangerter.

Huntsman eventually exited the race,[97] but Bangerter still trailed Wilson for the entirety of the contest until he finally pulled nearly even in polling during the final weekend of the campaign. On election night, Bangerter narrowly won with 40 percent of the vote to Wilson's 38 percent and Cook's 22 percent.

---

[96] The soon-to-be frontrunner in the 1992 governor's race had called for Bangerter to step aside and drop out of the 1988 race. This same candidate was defeated in his own run to replace Bangerter. The same goes for the heavyweight favorite in the 1992 U.S. Senate race who lost his election after commissioning his own poll in 1988 and staging a press conference to publicly tell Governor Bangerter he had no chance of winning. Political karma is real.
[97] As Huntsman prepared to exit the race, he wanted to communicate in person with Governor Bangerter. To avoid media scrutiny, Huntsman couldn't come to the Capitol and Bangerter couldn't come to his offices. The two instead met at an undisclosed LDS Church parking lot near the State Capitol to avoid detection.

Your path forward may look bleak, but every victorious campaign must always begin with hope. If Governor Bangerter can come back from impossible odds, so can you.

THE BOLERJACK RULE

Every campaign needs a closer.

During crunch time of critical games, longtime Utah Jazz announcer Craig Bolerjack frequently tells the crowd to "buckle up," as the two teams head to a rollercoaster finish. The universally beloved sportscaster even uses the Twitter handle @BuckleUpBoler.

The game of politics is no different. You will need a steady hand to take you across the finish line in a campaign. As polls tightens and campaigns get more desperate, a race can get ugly and candidates often behave in ways they end up regretting later. Overreaction or reacting to the wrong thing are hallmarks of these losing campaigns.

Sleep is infrequent. Your work hours are around the clock, and everyone's nerves are shot. It is at this moment that you need someone close to you who won't get rattled. It is best to identify who this person is well in advance of the final stretch of a campaign. Keep them close at all times, especially during the campaign's critical moments when numerous decisions will need to be made.

CHAPTER 3

GOVERNING

THE GRANGER SECOND WARD RULE

Sometimes the issues you will be most remembered for are completely out of your control.

Having just taken office as Utah's new governor only one month earlier, George Clyde found himself in the middle of the worst prison riot in Utah history in early February 1957. On that day, 500 inmates rioted and took over the main building at the Point of the Mountain Prison. Taken as hostages was the entire Granger Second Ward church basketball team, with the riot breaking out in the middle of their game with prisoners.

The irony is not lost on Utahns that the biggest riot in state history would take place in the middle of a church basketball game.

Governor Clyde attempted to negotiate the release of the hostages, and the prisoners responded with 43 requests including "alleged mishandling of inmate funds by prison personnel, unfair procedures by the board of pardons, poor food, and poor overall working and living conditions. Among their suggestions for improvement were the establishment of a prison newspaper, better inmate organization, including an inmate council, and a prison chapel."[1]

Only in Utah would prisoners riot so they could have a chapel.

By the following morning, a full 12 hours later, the hostages would be freed and order was restored to the prison again. The highly volatile situation could have turned out far worse for the new governor's administration. And of course, several months later construction would begin on the new chapel, all built with voluntary prison labor.

Seldom do you get to control what are the most important issues you will deal with in public office. Lyndon B. Johnson wanted to focus on his Great Society. Instead, he was stuck in the middle of the Vietnam War. Governor Clyde wanted to focus on building water infrastructure. Instead, he spent one of his first days in office negotiating hostage releases of a local church basketball team.

Remember the Granger Second Ward Rule and do your best to prepare for the unexpected. Politics has a way of surprising even the best public servants.

---

[1] James B. Allen, *Still the Right Place: Utah's Second Half-century of Statehood, 1945-1995* (Provo, UT: Charles Redd Center for Western Studies, 2016), 116. Allen is one of the most prominent scholars of Utah history as a professor at Brigham Young University and former historian for the LDS Church. I highly recommend the book.

THE CARLENE WALKER PRINCIPLE

Utahns are very agreeable. They want to say yes.

This rule derives its name from former Utah State Senator Carlene Walker, one of the state's most respected legislators during her time in the Senate. According to research conducted by BYU Professor Adam Brown,[2] Walker had the lowest number of "no" votes of any legislator in the last decade, casting an opposing vote less than one percent of the time.

In reality, this is quite common in Utah. Few votes ever fail in the Legislature despite the record number of bills that are proposed year after year. According to research by Brown, Senate votes only fail at an average rate of 1-2 percent, and House votes fail 2-4 percent of the time.

Most surprising is how this translates across party lines, with Democratic bills passing at high rates with very few issues being decided along partisan lines. In fact, according to Brown's research, during the last decade more than 90 percent of legislators voted together. In 2017, the number reached an all-time high with 97 percent of Senators voting together on legislation.

Do not underestimate the agreeableness of residents of the Beehive State. Utahns want their elected leaders to find solutions. Predictably, those elected to represent them share the same sentiment.[3]

---

[2] Brown is one of my favorite Utah political experts. His quantitative analysis provides context that many of us often miss. Those with interest in politics should pick up a copy of any one of his books on the subject, especially *Utah Politics and Government: American Democracy among a Unique Electorate* and *Utah Politics Under the Dome: Representation and the Utah Legislature.*

[3] The same has also held true with gubernatorial vetoes. According to Brown, Governor Gary Herbert vetoed only 0.8 percent of bills, Governor Jon Huntsman 0.7 percent, Governor Olene Walker 1.9 percent, and Governor Mike Leavitt 1.6 percent.

THE FADEAWAY JUMPER COROLLARY

Utahns can be passive aggressive.

As a Utah Jazz fan, the play that always frustrated me during the late 1990s championship runs was the Karl Malone fadeaway jumper.[4] Here was the strongest man in the entire NBA settling for a fadeaway jump shot.

To Malone's credit, his proficiency with the shot showed his impeccable work ethic as he began his career as a poor jump shooter. And I suppose he had an argument that falling backwards somehow made it harder for an opposing player to block him. However, the shot represented such a passive play for a player with his unprecedented level of strength.

Similarly, many out-of-state politicos are frequently flummoxed by Utah's seemingly passive approach to politics.[5] What they don't easily notice is what's going on beneath the surface, including from time to time passive aggression.

If you don't listen carefully enough, you might miss your opponent's subtle undermining of your point. The passive aggressive nature of the state can create an environment ripe for whisper campaigns. Political gossip can easily spread without being rebutted.

In Utah politics, don't let the Fadeaway Jumper Corollary fool you. There's plenty going on underneath the surface.

---

[4] Another was Malone's free throw shots that followed a strange ritual of him whispering words to himself for several seconds before releasing the shot. No word if he was just trying to outdo Jeff Hornacek's odd face rubbing before shooting every free throw.
[5] Sun Tzu in his *Art of War* said, "In battle, there are not more than two methods of attack— the direct and the indirect; yet these two in combination give rise to an endless series of maneuvers." Utahns are masters of the indirect attack.

THE BRAMBO COROLLARY

In a state that values niceness, a little aggressiveness goes a long ways.

If you visit the office of Utah Senator Curt Bramble, you will find a framed poster of him dressed as a Rambo look-alike with the name "BRAMBO" in capital letters. The drawing was put together by the Utah League of Cities and Towns,[6] who for years created playful cartoons of every Utah legislator.

The Brambo reference is intended as a compliment to one of the most gifted legislators in Utah political history. One national group recently ranked the Utah County Republican as the second-most productive senator in the entire nation. If there is a heavy lift in the Utah Legislature, Bramble is almost always involved, often as the bill's sponsor.

In 2011, it was Bramble who stepped forward and negotiated a comprehensive immigration legislation that was celebrated across the country. In 2014, he sponsored a controversial proposal on the caucus-convention process. No matter how divisive the issue, the Utah County Senator has shown his willingness to step forward and guide the state towards a solution.

Because our interactions in Utah can be more passive than other areas in the country, a person who is assertive[7] can be surprisingly effective.[8] Bramble has the unique ability to aggressively bring divergent parties to sit down at a table to find a common solution. Call it aggressive consensus. It's the Brambo way.

---

[6] A political subdivision of the state.
[7] A 2005 *Salt Lake Tribune* profile of the popular Utah County Senator characterized him as "not-Utah nice." Longtime friend Stan Lockhart said that it helps to remember his background being born and raised in Chicago and wrestling for the University of Notre Dame.
[8] The aggressiveness should never veer into the territory of what I call the HOA President Rule, defined as someone who as soon as they get a little authority (as they suppose) begins to exercise that authority in ways that are demeaning to others.

THE 9/11 TRUTHER COROLLARY

Avoid only telling people what they want to hear.

In 2010, newly elected Congressman Jason Chaffetz was recorded discussing with a constituent a conspiracy theory that the 9/11 attack was an inside job by the U.S. government. When asked if the investigation should be reopened, Chaffetz responded in the private conversation, "Well, I know there's still a lot to learn about what happened and what didn't happen. We should be vigilant and continue to investigate that, absolutely."[9]

In the conversation, Chaffetz referenced a BYU physics professor who had recently been placed on administrative leave by the university for his research on the subject. "Well there's a lot we still need to learn. Of course we want to look into that issue, look at every aspect of it....Who was the BYU professor? Steve Jones, yeah, I've met with him. He's done some interesting work."[10]

The supposedly private conversation quickly went viral once a copy of the recording was shared on social media.[11] Immediately, Chaffetz indicated he did not believe that 9/11 was an inside job and the investigation into its causes should not be reopened. It would have been a lot easier had he said that the first time.

The lesson to be learned for aspiring politicians is simple: avoid telling people what they want to hear. Politicians do it all the time because they want to be liked, but bending the truth or your own personal views in order to be liked by a crowd is a recipe for disaster.

---

[9] Matt Canham, "Chaffetz skewered over 9/11 conspiracy comments." *Salt Lake Tribune*, 19 February 2010.
[10] Lee Davidson, "No conspiracy in 9/11 attack, Chaffetz clarifies"* *Deseret News*, 19 February 2010.
[11] I personally blame the Deep State.
*See the Clarification Corollary (p. 166).

THE SENATE VOTING RULE

Most work is accomplished in informal settings.

As a staff member to former U.S. Senator Bob Bennett, one of my favorite activities was to watch votes on C-SPAN. The process is quite informal, with Senators rarely sitting in their seats. Instead, they mill around talking to each other while the clerk works through the voting role.

It is also during these moments when most of the Senate's actual work gets accomplished. Every time we would discuss an issue that needed to be resolved with another member, Senator Bennett would say, "I'll talk to them on the floor." Sure enough, as I watched C-SPAN, he would make his way through the crowd of senators to talk with the specific member about the issue. I always tried to judge the other member's facial expressions to see how receptive they were to the ask.

Another U.S. Senator from Utah recorded the following about floor votes: "It is not readily apparent on the outside how much of the Senate's business can be done during a vote. Some of the most important work on legislation – finding supporters, eliminating problems and turning around opponents – occurs during votes on other bills. It is the one time every member of the Senate has to come to the well in the front of the chamber. Despite being in public, it is one of the few places where a senator can talk directly to a colleague without interruption."[12]

In the field of politics, a lot of work can be accomplished during informal settings. The nature of the work and number of parties often involved makes it very difficult to schedule one-on-one meetings with everyone. Instead, find opportunities where you can interact with others during informal settings to help advance your goals.

---

[12] Orrin Hatch, *Square Peg: Confessions of a Citizen Senator* (New York: Basic Books, 2003), 34.

THE CHUCK-A-RAMA RULE

Pick a niche. Trying to be all things to all people seldom works.

Any time I go to a restaurant that tries to be more than one thing, I'm almost always disappointed (e.g. a Mexican restaurant that also serves hamburgers).[13] With the lone exception of the popular Utah buffet Chuck-A-Rama, it is impossible to be all things to all people.[14]

Politics isn't all that different. If you want to pursue public service at virtually any level of government, it is critical that you choose a focus. Those who don't follow this practice frequently find themselves lacking direction.

A newly elected city council member could choose to focus on transportation infrastructure. An aspiring state legislator might want to be the expert on education funding. But whatever you do, please choose. Your time in office will be far more successful if you do.

After all, in politics you can do anything you want, but you can't do everything.

---

[13] I recommend you visit Victor's Tires and Tamales at 1406 South 700 West in Salt Lake City for an excellent (and unusual) dining experience. The odd combination began years ago as the tire shop began offering chips and salsa to waiting customers. Today, there is an entire dining area adjacent to the store, although you still have to order your food in the tire shop.
[14] Kudos to Matt Whitlock, the brilliant communications director for U.S. Senator Orrin Hatch, for the frequent publicized visits of Senator Hatch to Chuck-A-Rama. It cracks me up every time.

THE BEN WINSLOW COROLLARY

Focus on areas where no one else is paying attention.

Once called by another political commentator "The greatest tweeter in the Intermountain West," Ben Winslow never lacks for dedication to his craft.

But even more than the volume of news coverage Winslow is able to generate, it's the attention to details that others often overlook that makes him such an excellent reporter.

During my time working for Utah Governor Gary Herbert, we would always prepare a collection of potential questions that the governor might be asked during his monthly KUED press conference. The event was broadcast live with any reporter in the state able to attend. Any question was considered fair play.

To prepare, we would compile information about the issues of the day, and almost always we could predict the kinds of questions the governor would be asked. There was only one exception, Ben Winslow. Because of his attention to even the smallest of details on a few specific issues in the state, we had a section of the governor's prep dedicated just to him. For example, I don't know of another reporter who attends every single Department of Alcoholic Beverage Control meeting.[15]

The Winslow Corollary is also a good reminder to politicians. It's not enough just to focus on specific issues. Sometimes focusing on the areas that everyone else is ignoring and swimming upstream can be tremendously rewarding.

---

[15] Winslow has been known to say, "Because if it's booze, it's news." He also recently received an award from the Society of Professional Journalists in the category, "Best Marijuana Reporting."

THE BENGHAZI COROLLARY

A singular focus is important, but too much attention to only one issue eventually grows old.

Outside of Utah circles, this rule is referred to as "Captain Ahabing," named after the antagonist in Herman Melville's book, *Moby Dick*. For 544 pages,[16] Captain Ahab was singularly obsessed with a white whale, a passion that ultimately led to his demise.

Utah Congressman Jason Chaffetz (R-Los Gatos) devoted a significant amount of attention to the important issue of the U.S. government's response to the disaster in Benghazi. However, his obsession with the subject at the expense of any other issue eventually made for a frustrated public. Even those who appreciated the Congressman's focus on the scandal began to wonder if his singular obsession was preventing him from working on other important issues.[17]

Be focused, but becoming obsessed with only one issue can make you appear to be out of balance.[18]

---

[16] I call it the Martin Harris Rule whenever a book wouldn't lose any quality if it was 116 pages shorter. *Moby Dick* tops this list for me. Also, you can find an inside look at the Benghazi scandal on page 116 (and pretty much every page) of Chaffetz's new book, *The Deep State: How an Army of Bureaucrats Protected Barack Obama and Is Working to Destroy the Trump Agenda*.

[17] I also considered naming this the Zucchini Rule. Something that is otherwise useful can become annoying at a certain point.

[18] *Out of Balance* is also the title of Governor Scott Matheson's excellent book on the need to restore federalism.

THE BOB BERNICK RULE

Learn the rules and procedures of political institutions.

When I served in the Utah House of Representatives, one of my favorite legislative assignments was on the Rules Committee, an important body that referred all legislation to various standing committees. The work was as inside baseball as it gets in the Legislature with committee meetings held during House floor time and often for only a few minutes at a time.

And yet every time our committee met, there in attendance was one reporter (and almost always only one reporter), Bob Bernick. One of Utah's most experienced journalists, Bernick is a *Utah Policy* contributing editor and former *Deseret News* columnist. Almost no one in the Utah press corps has as much experience in the trenches of Utah politics, which shows in his unique style of political commentary.

If you want to succeed in politics either as an elected official or other contributing party, you need to understand the rules of the process. If you have a knowledge of these sometimes arcane rules, it presents you with significant influence over your peers. Learn the ins and outs of the budgeting process, or what motions are in order and in what precedence. The more you know, the more influence you will obtain.

THE CAL BLACK RULE

Utahns have an inherent distrust of the federal government.[19]

As one of Utah's founders of the Sagebrush Rebellion, San Juan County Commissioner Cal Black was virulently opposed to federal management of public lands and any expansion of wilderness protections. He also served as mayor of Blanding,[20] and a member of the Utah Legislature. Years later one of Utah's most prominent political thinkers said the former rural leader reminded him of, "Mike Noel on steroids." Black is perhaps best known as the inspiration for the antagonist "Bishop Love" in Edward Abbey's bestselling novel *The Monkey Wrench Gang.*[21]

With much of a rural community's livelihood tied to public lands, it should not surprise many Utahns that they would continually elect someone who would take such strong stands on public lands issues. Nearly two-thirds of the state's land is managed by the federal government, with a persistent tension between factions.[22]

---

[19] It doesn't help that the federal government specifically chose rural Nevada as a testing ground for nuclear weapons testing because the prevailing wind would take radioactive debris towards southern Utah, a place classified documents at the time called "a low-use segment of the population."

[20] The town of Blanding was originally known as Grayson until 1914 when a rich easterner, Thomas Bicknell, offered to give any Utah town a thousand-book collection if they changed their name to Bicknell. Two towns agreed to the offer and split the library of books which brought about the name change for the Utah town Bicknell (previously Thurber) and Blanding (the maiden name of Bicknell's wife). The *Utah History Encyclopedia* records that residents of the town were upset that the books were in poor condition.

[21] The book's character clearly shows the author's disdain for Black's politics, but he also wrote a letter to a sick Black in 1988 saying, "Dear Cal, I hear rumors that you've come down with a serious illness. If true, I hope you beat it. Although you and I probably disagree about almost everything, you should know that I have never felt the slightest ill will toward you as a person. Furthermore, you still owe me an airplane ride. Good luck and best wishes. Ed Abbey." Buckley Jensen, "Remarkable life from humble start," *San Juan Record*, 1 October 2008.

[22] Utahns frequently complain of federal interference on public lands, but they also have been quick to hold out a hand to federal coffers for important water development projects.

THE MIKE MOWER PRINCIPLE

Always remember the little things.

In a world that seems to spin constantly faster and faster, it is a rare thing to have a politico who steps back and takes the time to remember the simple, little things. No one demonstrates this better than Mike Mower, Ferron native and deputy chief of staff to Utah Governor Gary Herbert.

Countless Utahns receive text messages from him as he travels to every town in the state, large or small. Usually the message includes a photo of Mower next to something important to the recipient of the message. He remembers something you said in a previous conversation and takes the time to show he cares about you by snapping a picture.

A lot of success in politics can be attributed to just showing up. Mower will do this with Utahns from across the state. No town is too small. No organization too unimportant. One time I received a phone call from my parents in rural Utah who said, "The nicest man stopped by today." Of course, it was Mike Mower.

As a candidate, when you win it is amazing to see the flood of phone calls and text messages congratulating you on the victory. But for those who are struggling through an election defeat or a round of bad press, it is equally amazing to see how silent your phone will be. With the exception of one call: Mike Mower.[23]

Too many people check in only when they need something. Not Mower. Without a doubt, he is one of the nicest human beings you will ever meet.

---

[23] I remember the day after the *Salt Lake Tribune* published a story about several Utah politicos engaged in a scandal. My phone was buzzing with messages from other insiders gleefully celebrating the news. I walked into Mower's office, just as he was getting off the phone with one of the individuals caught up in the scandal. I asked him what he was doing, and he said, "Everybody remembers you when you're up, but they all forget you when you're down."

If the maxim "Nice guys finish last" was true, Mower would not have enjoyed such longevity in Utah politics.

Politics has a way of changing quickly. The losers of today can be the winners tomorrow. Remember the Mike Mower Rule next time you are tempted to gossip about the person who is down on their luck.

The world would be a better place if more people practiced politics the way that Mike Mower does.[24] He is an example to any aspiring politician about the right way to make your way to the top.

---

[24] You won't find a kinder person than Mike Mower. After my car was stolen from in front of the governor's mansion on a Friday afternoon, "Uber Mike" was there waiting at my curb Monday morning to take me into the office. I never asked for the ride. He just showed up.

THE ARTHUR WATKINS RULE

Always stand up for your values, even if it costs you a failed reelection bid.

Unknown to many Utahns, Orem-native Arthur Watkins played a prominent role in the downfall of former U.S. Senator Joseph McCarthy as chair of the Senate Select Committee that recommended his censure.[25]

McCarthy supporters across the country, including many Utahns, were outraged by the work of Watkins and the committee's reprimand of the popular Wisconsin Senator. Expressing his anger at the treatment of McCarthy, former Utah Governor J. Bracken Lee announced his challenge to the incumbent Senator Watkins in his upcoming reelection.[26]

Watkins defeated Lee in the Republican primary, but Lee chose to continue his challenge as an independent in the general election.[27] While ultimately unsuccessful, political insiders agree that his split of Republicans helped Democrat Frank Moss ultimately prevail. In one of the most closely contested three-way races in Utah history, Moss won (36 percent), followed by Watkins (33 percent) and Lee (31 percent). Had Watkins been less critical of Senator McCarthy, he likely could have won.

Every public leader is faced at one point or another with decisions that could end your political career. When in doubt, remember the Arthur Watkins Rule and do the right thing. You may lose your reelection, but you will never be ashamed of your decision.

---

[25] Little-known trivia about Watkins is that he was also the father-in-law of LDS Apostle Richard G. Scott.

[26] There is a degree of irony in Lee's anti-Communist push since he would later be fiercely criticized for his firing of prominent anti-Communist Cleon Skousen as Salt Lake City police chief. I would quote several passages from Skousen's famous book, *The Naked Communist*, but Senator Todd Weiler has deemed it to be a public health crisis.

[27] Back in 1958, a candidate could lose as a Republican before choosing to run as an independent. Today, a candidate has to choose one or the other at the beginning of the campaign cycle. U.S. Senator Bob Bennett called this change the J. Bracken Lee Rule.

THE SHARKNADO RULE

Do something a little unexpected.

In 2016, Governor Gary Herbert was in the middle of a tough reelection campaign, ultimately losing at the Republican state convention before crushing his opponent in the primary election. With a challenger and a bullseye on his back, every decision was vetted with extra care.

Around this same time, I had a strange request from Salt Lake FanX leaders. Would Governor Herbert be willing to act as an extra in a taping of *Sharknado 4* to be filmed in conjunction with their annual convention? As his communications director, I sheepishly presented the idea to the governor and he immediately responded, "Sure."[28]

The script called for the governor to use a baseball bat to fight off sharks trying to invade the state's Capitol building. We improvised on the spot and instead decided to use a tennis racket, the governor's preferred sport.[29] For months to come, everywhere we went someone would ask us about the cameo with a smile on their face. They seemed to appreciate a politician who didn't take himself too seriously.

Consistency is tremendously valuable in Utah politics, but never become too predictable. People still like the occasional surprise.

---

[28] In my defense, I also made sure the movie wouldn't be released until after the primary election.

[29] All in all, the taping only took 15 minutes of the governor's time.

THE FAXING UNDERWEAR COROLLARY

Being unpredictable should never cross into the zone of erratic behavior.

In a November 1998 email to fellow staff members, the just-fired chief of staff to former Congressman Merrill Cook warned of his progressively odd behavior by saying, "If he asks you to fax his underwear to the speaker's office, please just do it."[30]

The person continued by writing that the congressman was having "some kind of psychotic breakdown....Merrill has taken up permanent residence in wacko land, and we are all in serious jeopardy."[31]

The supposedly private email message ended up in the hands of members of the media, and the story of an erratic Congressman became the brand most associated with Cook, eventually leading to his undoing in a 2000 primary loss to fellow Republican Derek Smith.

Cook was never able to really shed that image. He described the emails as the actions of a disgruntled, now-former employee, but in the world of politics perception is often greater than reality, and the image stuck.

A *Deseret News* profile piece years after he had left office started like this, "Mention the name of Merrill Cook and people tend to roll their eyes. See, you're doing it now as you read this. Crazy Merrill."[32]

Fair or not, the lesson is clear: being unpredictable can be a political asset, but cross the line into erratic territory and your political future will undoubtedly be limited.

---

[30] Lee Davidson, "More charges fly of erratic behavior by Merrill Cook." *Deseret News*, 19 November 1998.
[31] Ibid.
[32] Doug Robinson, "Cook's task: rebuild his life." *Deseret News*, 13 March 2005.

THE MIMI'S CAFÉ PRINCIPLE

Some Utahns can be gullible.

In 2009, a rumor started that Michael Jordan was going to play Bryon Russell[33] in a one-on-one game during halftime of a Utah Flash basketball game.

"It was a less-than-fulfilling culmination of months of speculation – most of it fueled by the Utah Flash and its owner Brandt Andersen[34] – that Jordan would face off with Russell in what would be a re-enactment of the final basket[35] of the 1998 NBA Finals."[36]

One of the highlights of the whole episode came from a video posted by an anonymous YouTube user (the Utah Flash later admitted it was their video), supposedly of a Michael Jordan sighting at a Utah County Mimi's Cafe before the game.

Let's suspend reality for a moment and pretend that Jordan's ego is just big enough that he can't reject a challenge, no matter the source. So he

---

[33] We all remember the demeaning comment from Michael Jordan during the 1997 NBA Finals when he purposefully called Bryon Russell, "Byron." This is especially confusing for some Utahns who have gotten to know the actual Byron Russell, a former executive at Zions Bank and all-around great guy.

[34] My favorite quote from Anderson: "We've had some conversations, and I think there's a good possibility that he's going to be here. He'll say no he's not. If you ask him straight on he'll say no he won't. If you ask his people they'll say no he won't. You know what, I've probably said too much. But I think there's a good chance he might be here. Let's leave it at that."*
Henry Abbott, "The Michael Jordan isn't real and neither is Santa." *ESPN*, 8 December 2009.

[35] The Jordan Pushoff Rule of politics is that you should not underestimate the power of incumbency. The best NBA players get preferential treatment from officials, and the same is often true of political incumbents.

[36] Darnell Dickson, "Michael Jordan's supposed appearance at Flash game was a hoax." *Daily Herald*, 8 December 2009.

* There is certainly a lot to ponderize in this quote.

comes to the state and chooses to eat at Mimi's Cafe?[37] Sirens should be going off in the minds of anyone following the story at this point in time.

Apparently some people actually bought into the hype, as a sellout crowd showed up for the Flash game that night. I received multiple calls from friends asking if I wanted to attend with them.[38] At halftime, Russell walked out of one tunnel, but it quickly became obvious that the man coming out of the other tunnel and surrounded by guards was not Michael Jordan but a look-alike of the NBA star. Russell left and that was the end of the production.

Isn't America great?[39] The fake Michael Jordan charade in Utah County easily constitutes one of my top 10 underappreciated Utah news stories of the decade.[40] Of course, furious fans booed their hearts out when they realized they had been conned.[41]

We see it in other aspects of life in the Beehive State. Nefarious business leaders have used this same innate trust that Utahns have to swindle them out of money. Political leaders are not immune either.[42] Essentially it comes down to one simple truism. In Utah, we want to believe you. We're a trusting people. Some unscrupulous politicians may take advantage of this fact, but by and large they don't.

---

[37] The obvious restaurant choice in Utah County should have been Oregano Italian Kitchen with its extraordinary chef and owner Chad Pritchard. As a last resort, he could have always stopped in Pleasant Grove at the Purple Turtle.

[38] Most of those same friends have subsequently invited me to make hundreds of thousands of dollars as part of their latest summer sales scheme.

[39] Again.

[40] There are so many angles of the story that deserve to be explored. How did the owner of the Flash ever think this would be a good idea? What was his best-case scenario? How does one go about finding a Michael Jordan look-alike?

[41] The official apology after the fact from the Flash owner is another gem: "I knew I would not know if MJ was going to attend until a few hours before game time. I never received the call indicating he would not attend. Which was to be expected with the mighty Air Jordan." Henry Abbott, "The Michael Jordan isn't real and neither is Santa." *ESPN*, 8 December 2009.

[42] See the Douglas Stringfellow Theory (p. 178).

THE SALT PUMP WARNING

You are more likely to be remembered for a large capital project than any other policy initiative.

At the end of his two terms in office in 1991, a poll asked Utahns what they believed Governor Norm Bangerter would be remembered for in years to come. It was an open-ended poll, and yet a remarkable 52 percent said he would be remembered for the Great Salt Lake pumps, an innovative, albeit never-used pump that would move water out into Utah's west desert in case of flooding. The next highest issue came in at only 6 percent (balanced budget). Even more surprising was the fact that the pumps were built during Bangerter's first year in office, yet Utahns still remembered after he left office seven years later.[43]

Anyone involved in Utah politics has heard the joke. "I wonder if this will be the year when we'll finally need Governor Bangerter's water pumps." Bangerter steered the state through enormously difficult times, including a significant recession and budget deficit. But despite his many achievements, the pumps were what people remembered.[44] Before engaging in a large capital project, do your homework.[45] Those physical reminders of your work stay around forever.[46]

---

[43] To be fair, it was former Governor Scott Matheson who actually came up with the idea for the pumps. Matheson was also the source of one of my favorite quotes from a Utah political leader. During the catastrophic 1983 floods, he said, "This is one helluva way to run a desert." Dale Russakoff, "As Utah Melts, Masses of Mud Are on the Move." *Washington Post*, 26 May 1984.

[44] One of the more creative bumper stickers came from this election, courtesy of Utah Democrats: "Pump Norm to the West Desert."

[45] Some politicians take advantage of this natural hesitation to build large capital projects by pointing to potential major problems that may occur. My favorite was a response to the proposed Utah State Prison relocation. The Salt Lake City mayor at that time warned that building the state prison so near the Great Salt Lake could endanger the structure in the event of a possible tsunami.

[46] Don't be the elected official who puts a big plaque with your name on it in the new public building. I think if these plaques were removed, it would cut our building fund needs in the state by half.

THE WALLACE GARDNER THEORY

Your success in political office is often dependent on other people with whom you serve.

In what amounts to the Davis County version of the Eastonian Rule (p. 32). Governor Cal Rampton grew up in his Bountiful home next to the family of Governor Charles Mabey.[47] In his memoirs, *As I Recall*, Rampton shared the following story:

> I have a vivid recollection of a day that fell within a day or two of my seventh birthday. That morning I noticed there was a great deal of activity at the Mabey house. I went through the back lot to the Mabey house and into the back door without knocking, as always, and I found Bob in the kitchen and asked him to come out and play. He said he couldn't, that he wanted to see all the people. I asked him why so many people were there and he said, "My father has just been elected governor."
>
> "What's a governor?"
>
> And Bob said, "He's the boss of the whole state."
>
> That was a statement I would later find was a great exaggeration.[48]

---

[47] Mabey's opponent in the 1924 race, George Dern, wins the award for best campaign slogan in state history: "We want a Dern good governor, and we don't mean Mabey."* My other honorable mention was the 2004 election team of Scott Matheson Jr. (governor) and Karen Hale (lieutenant governor). They chose not to pursue the slogan, but a finalist from suggestions they publicly released was "Hale Yes, Vote Matheson."

[48] Calvin L. Rampton, Floyd A. O'Neil, and Gregory C. Thompson, *As I Recall* (Salt Lake City: University of Utah Press, 1989), 10.

*If you really want to impress your friends, remind them that Governor Charles Mabey was also a published poet. Next time you're in the special collections of the Utah State Archives, ask for Box 2 of the Mabey collection for an inside look at the former governor's poems.

In reflecting upon his time as Utah's longest serving governor, Cal Rampton took special note to acknowledge one person to whom he felt particularly indebted to for his success: Wallace Gardner, a Republican from Utah County.

The fact that Rampton, a Democrat, would give so much credit to a member of the opposing political party may seem surprising. However, the way that Rampton recalled their relationship was as follows, "If we had a problem where we appraised a matter differently, we could generally sit down and talk it out. I feel that I owe a great deal to that man because he helped me make my administration a financially responsible one."[49]

Politicians are seldom humble enough to acknowledge this critical point. Your success or failure as a public leader is often determined by not only your own actions but those of your peers as well.

That first day you're sworn in to the city council or state legislature, look around you at the other men and women standing next to you. Your success will largely depend on your ability to work together.[50]

---

[49] Ibid, 213.
[50] Rampton's brother Byron also found himself in an awkward position serving alongside Gardner as a Republican state senator at the same time his Democrat brother was governor.

THE LARRY H. MILLER CREDIT CARD THEORY

You can cry in Utah politics.

In John Stockton's 2009 Hall of Fame acceptance speech, he related the following story:

"Larry Miller, our team owner, used to start crying when he talked a lot and he'd take a credit card and kind of scrape the tears off his face and just keep plowing through."[51]

Larry H. Miller was not the only Utahn quick to tears, often in endearing ways.[52] Former Utah Senate President and Salt Lake Chamber President Lane Beattie was well known for his penchant for tears. Compare that to the national example of former House Speaker John Boehner who was often mocked for even brief episodes of crying.[53]

Perhaps part of the reason why Utahns have a high tolerance and even affection for the occasional tear from its leaders is because of the semiannual general conference of the LDS Church, the state's predominant faith. It is common for church leaders to be moved to tears in a speech. Ultimately they compose themselves and finish their message, but an occasional tear is not seen as a leadership weakness.

---

[51] "Sloan, Stockton Hall of Fame Acceptance Speeches," *KSL.com*, 14 September 2009.
[52] The H. in Larry H. Miller was always used because when he first went to register his business in Utah, another "Larry Miller" had already registered the business name. If you ever feel like you'll never make it in Utah politics, try to imagine what a 35-year old Larry Miller must have felt like when he went to register that first business as an unknown Utahn.
[53] Presidential candidate Ed Muskie saw his candidacy take an abrupt turn for the worse when he broke into tears during a 1972 press conference. Political insiders credit this moment for the beginning of his demise in the race. Muskie's campaign blamed the episode not on tears but "melted snow."

THE RICK MAJERUS RULE

In politics, everything is better with food.

You want happy campaign volunteers? Show up with pizza. You want better attendance at your town hall? Bring treats.[54] No one epitomized this rule better than legendary University of Utah basketball coach Rick Majerus.[55]

A little humorous to think about in retrospect, the University of Utah was actually put on official probation by the NCAA for Majerus's penchant for eating out with players and providing milk and cookies at team film sessions.

Always good for a quote, Majerus had this to say to a *Salt Lake Tribune* reporter about his love of food: "I'm particularly happy to go back to Chicago. I mean, we don't have an Italian restaurant in Utah that ends in a vowel. [In Utah], you're eating at a place like Olson's or something and ordering baked manicotti out of the Chef Boyardee can."

Whether it's a busy night at campaign headquarters or your visit to the Carbon County convention, remember that everything is better with a little food.

---

[54] Former Utah Representative Rick Wheeler would arrive at delegates' homes with a fresh loaf of homemade bread. Mitt Romney said his favorite meat is hot dog, a food he frequently shared on the campaign trail, not to be confused with the famous Romney family dog Seamus who has an entire Wikipedia entry dedicated to him.

[55] While not a politician, Majerus did file to run for the Utah State Board of Education in 1992. He made it through the first round of nominees but was not appointed by Governor Norm Bangerter. In his autobiography, *My Life on a Napkin*, the Utah coach related a conversation he once had with U.S. Senator Orrin Hatch. Hatch told him, "If you ever want to do anything politically, run for office, you've got a friend here" (p. 61). Jon Huntsman Sr. said of Majerus, "I think Rick has been an everyday event in my life. He's clearly the dearest, most trusted friend outside of my own family that I have on the earth today" (p. 64).

THE QUAKING ASPEN THEORY

Your most important work frequently gets the least amount of attention.

We spend a lot of time in political bodies debating unimportant issues because we understand them, while ignoring debate on important issues because we don't understand them. This theory is also true of the public and not just politicians.

This theory gets its name from the vigorous debate that took place in the 2014 Utah State Legislature regarding the naming of a new state tree, the quaking aspen.[56] The state had previously adopted the Colorado Blue Spruce. Other issues received little to no attention from the general public, but the state tree received top billing.

Similarly, every local government adopts an annual budget. In virtually every jurisdiction, not a single member of the public shows up to express their views on the millions of dollars in expenditures. However, the entire town will mobilize if the city tries to relocate a deer wandering through town.[57]

A craven political leader may actively seek controversial items of minor importance in order to distract from the weightier issues being debated. The spotlight is subsequently moved.[58] Typically this chasing of shining objects occurs all on its own and without manipulation.

Remember that the issues of most interest to the public are not always the most important to your work as an elected leader.

---

[56] Multiple legislators remarked that this was the first time they finally got respect from their young children who had recently studied Utah history in elementary school.
[57] That one was for my many friends in Draper.
[58] Affectionately known as the Wag the Dog Rule.

THE CARL WIMMER RULE

Never trust a politician with a mustache.

There are no exceptions to this rule. [59]

---

[59] With the exception of Utah Representatives Lee Perry and Scott Chew. As far as I can tell, there is no honor code on facial hair for male Utah politicians. However, seldom if ever do you see someone with a beard running for statewide office. It is common for a candidate to grow out a beard after losing a race or announcing their retirement. Mostly I'm just joking about the rule, and significant praise goes out to Wimmer for his work helping struggling rural youth in his post-legislative career. He has made Sanpete County a far better place thanks to his selfless service.

THE DAVID B. HAIGHT RULE

Avoid being too scripted.

In 1976, President Gerald Ford delivered a speech to the American public, which included this memorable line, "And I say to you, this is nonsense with emphasis."

His written speech used the phrase "with emphasis" in the margins to encourage him to make a point of the sentence. But Ford instead read the words out loud. As former Texas Governor Rick Perry would say, "Oops."

This robotic delivery can frequently be seen when LDS leaders use a teleprompter for the first time to give remarks during the faith's general conference. Some of the most gifted speakers almost always struggle through that first speech. Compare that to former church leader David B. Haight[60] who notably had such poor eyesight that he couldn't use the same teleprompter system. Inevitably, audiences always paid more attention to his speeches because you were never quite sure what he might say. The chance for an off-script moment was high, and you didn't want to miss it.

Some of the most memorable speeches (for better or worse) are those where the candidate goes off script. There is inevitable risk associated with this strategy, but one of the most underestimated skills in politics is authenticity. Be yourself.

---

[60] Haight had his own political background as mayor of Palo Alto, California. He is also the grandfather to former Utah Governor Jon Huntsman Jr.

THE "I BROUGHT THESE AWARDS" RULE

Never use your position in public office to try and get out of trouble.

In 2017, congressional candidate and former State Representative Chris Herrod was caught speeding down I-15. During the initial stop, he stated, "I'm a former legislator that was honored. I'm happy to go on my credibility."[61] The officer dismissed the comment and wrote him a ticket.

Rather than pay the speeding ticket, the candidate appeared before a judge two months later to fight his case. While presenting his side of the story, the former legislator brought forward several awards he had received during his time as an elected official. He told the judge, "I brought these awards. They're all from the highway patrol. Not that they'd get me out of anything but simply to say that I don't have a police issue."[62]

When the story became public, the candidate quickly apologized for his behavior and moved on. If elected to public office, never say the words, "Do you know who I am?" Never invoke your time as an elected leader in hopes that you might get off easy. And never bring awards to a court hearing with a judge.[63]

---

[61] Tamara Vaifanua, 3rd Congressional candidate fights traffic ticket; apologizes for courtroom behavior." *Fox 13 News*, 28 July 2017.
[62] Ibid.
[63] And a word to the wise, always pay for pizza delivery with cash only.

THE MARRIOTT GLOBES PRINCIPLE

Utahns feel a strong connection to the rest of the world. Nativist policies don't work here.

If you ever get a spare moment, take a moment to visit the Grand Reading Room on the third floor of the University of Utah's Marriott Library, overlooking Rice-Eccles Stadium. As you enter that room, you will come across two large globes, each of them three feet in diameter. One is a traditional globe showing the various countries of the world, while the other shows the stars and constellations of the sky. They are likely the biggest globes you have ever seen, two of only eight globes of their kind left in the world today. Each was made in the 19th century out of paper mache and painted with watercolors, a monumental task at the time.

So, why are they sitting there in the middle of the University of Utah library?

Upon the organization of the University of Deseret in 1850, university officials asked that they be purchased from London, the only place you could buy such things at that time. From there, Franklin D. Richards brought the two gigantic globes across the vast Atlantic Ocean and began the slow wagon ride across the plains to the desert valley of Utah. Upon arrival after months and months of strenuous travel, the globes would be proudly displayed at the university for years to come. Professors would take their students to see them. The globes were prominently featured in the city's Fourth of July parade.[64] They even wheeled them out each year for the annual state fair and other similar occasions.

---

[64] Historian Will Bagley found that two separate Fourth of July* celebrations were held in Utah until 1887 when a unified event occurred, including one instance when church leaders flew American flags at half-staff to protest federal polygamy laws.

*In the rotunda of the Utah State Capitol is a mural of the Dominguez-Escalante Expedition, the first Europeans to explore Utah. Ironically, the planned departure date for the expedition was July 4, 1776, celebrated today as our nation's Independence Day.

Such wear and tear is perhaps best seen if you look close enough at where the state of Utah should be located. The spot has essentially been blotted out, not by rain or snow or other accidents, but by constant rubbing of fingers by both children and adults pointing out their Utah home. [65]

Despite being founded in a place intended to be left alone by the rest of country, Utahns have always felt a strong desire to be connected to the world. Nativism doesn't work here. Free trade is encouraged. Missionaries return from all corners of the world speaking more languages than any other state in America. Our young children attend dual immersion schools and learn of different cultures across the globe. Our governors welcome refugees from war-torn areas of the world.

In short, nativism doesn't work in the Beehive State.

---

[65] Credit should be given to Overstock.com executive Patrick Byrne who donated funds to help restore the globes to be showcased again to residents of the state.

THE TOPAZ COROLLARY

Utahns are not immune from discriminatory behavior.

After the December 1941 Pearl Harbor attack, President Franklin D. Roosevelt ordered all Japanese residents (including citizens) to be forcibly placed in internment camps. One of the nation's largest camps was located in Millard County at a site known as Topaz. The approximately 11,000 internees held at Topaz were uprooted from their homes and sent to their new desert home, which at the time represented the largest city in all of Millard County. The camp would eventually close in 1945 at the conclusion of the war.

Frank Ogawa was one of these American citizens of Japanese descent who was forcibly interned at Topaz. After the war, he and his family settled in Oakland, California where he would become the first Japanese-American to be elected to a major city council in the continental United States. He would serve for 28 years on the Oakland City Council, the longest tenure in the city's history.

While Utah has a proud history of religious and ethnic tolerance, it also has a history of discrimination towards other groups like the Japanese in World War II. Current trends have seen members of the state stand up to bigotry and racism, but it is no guarantee that the state will continue down this path without strong leadership willing to stand up to those who believe otherwise. [66]

---

[66] If you visit the Utah State Capitol today, you will find 433 cherry trees surrounding the majestic building. Each spring, Utahns from across the state come to visit these beautiful trees in full bloom. According to the Capitol Preservation Board, the Japanese gifted the trees to the state as a symbol of reconciliation and friendship after World War II. Perhaps it is time we offer a similar gesture and plant cherry trees near the site of Utah's Topaz internment camp.

THE REVA BECK BOSONE RULE

There is strength in numbers.

Bosone was the first Utah woman to serve as a member of Congress. Elected in 1948, Bosone performed better than fellow Democrat Harry Truman on the Utah ballot.[67] This was the culmination of many firsts for the prominent Utah public official. She was also the first female majority leader in the Utah House of Representatives, and later became the first female judge in the state.[68]

Soon after her election to Congress,[69] Bosone was among only four members of the House of Representatives to vote against the Central Intelligence Agency Act. Bosone opposed the newly-formed agency due to its lack of transparency and congressional oversight. Her opponent in the 1952 election would use this vote against her, arguing that Bosone was a Communist sympathizer. The nation was in the middle of Cold War hysteria, and the label stuck. Bosone was defeated.[70]

During your time in office, there will be frequent tough votes and decisions you will have to make. Where possible, building coalitions of support will help you explain a difficult position to your constituents. Always vote your conscience, but never forget that there is strength in political numbers.

---

[67] Bosone credited her mother for her early interest in politics. She reported that her mother taught her, "If you want to do good, you go where the laws are made because a country is no better than its laws."

[68] Speaking about the issue of sexism in politics, Bosone said, "Generally speaking, men who refuse to recognize a qualified woman on their staff or as their opponent or in public office suffer from an inferiority complex. Show me an intelligent man and I'll show you a fair-minded one."

[69] Bosone's campaign slogan was, "Yes! A Woman!"

[70] A *Utah History Encyclopedia* entry about Bosone mentioned that she spent the years between her retirement and 1983 death enjoying her family and encouraging women to "raise more hell."

THE UTAH COMPACT COROLLARY

Build alliances to push forward a controversial initiative.

Utahns and members of the LDS faith have been celebrated in recent years for their stand in support of Muslims and refugees. However, the state nearly fell into a much different narrative on immigration several years ago.

Arizona State Senator Russell Pearce sponsored a controversial show-your-papers legislation in 2010. Many remember the Arizona law, but they don't remember that Pearce and many of the bill's most outspoken supporters were members of the Church of Jesus Christ of Latter-day Saints.

Following the Arizona bill, several Utah legislators planned to push for similar legislation in Utah, when business and church leaders from across the state stepped forward to propose what they called the Utah Compact. This set of key immigration principles set forth a welcoming immigration policy for the state.

Today, the narrative on Utah being a state that encourages immigration is accepted as the norm, but in 2010 the issue was very much in doubt. The Utah Compact completely changed the narrative by seizing the initiative and forcing anti-immigration legislators to play defense. Leaders of the Salt Lake Chamber deserve considerable credit for such a noteworthy achievement. And as always, Senator Curt Bramble was there leading the way and sponsoring the bill. It made me proud to be a Utahn.

When you face long odds and an uncertain path forward, follow the Utah Compact Corollary and assemble a strong coalition of community supporters. The broad-based effort will be much more effective than going it alone.

THE BEVERLY TAYLOR SORENSON RULE

Utahns value the arts.

Despite being a predominantly Republican state, Utah has a proud history of supporting the arts. The pioneers arrived in 1847 with local plays being performed almost immediately upon their arrival. The city's Social Hall was completed in 1853 with the Deseret Dramatic Association holding numerous performances in the new hall with seating for 300 patrons. A bust of William Shakespeare was kept on the stage.

Only a few years later in 1862, Brigham Young[71] led the effort to construct the massive Salt Lake Theatre.[72] Even though the 1860 census only estimated Salt Lake City's population to be approximately 8,000, the theatre's capacity was estimated to be 1,500.[73]

Today, the arts maintain similar prominence in the Beehive State. Nearly every day, one of my three daughters comes home from their elementary school excited about their latest art or music project. Rather than being

---

[71] Young famously remarked, "If I were placed on a cannibal island and given a task of civilizing its people, I should straightway build a theater." Leonard J. Arrington, *Brigham Young: American Moses* (Urbana, IL: University of Illinois Press, 1986), 290.

[72] Young's lone acting performance occurred in the 1844 Nauvoo, Illinois performance of *Pizarro*. Young played the role of a Peruvian priest in the performance. A playbill of the performance was discovered more than 100 years later by the Missouri Historical Society. The purpose of the play was described in the playbill, "To aid in the discharge of a debt, against President Joseph Smith, contracted through the odious persecution of Missouri, and vexatious law suits. His friends and the public will respond to so laudable a call, in patronising [sic] the exertions of those who promise rational amusement with the usefulness." Stanley B. Kimball, "Also Starring Brigham Young." *Ensign*, October 1975.

[73] A Massachusetts editor said of the theater, "No eastern city of one hundred thousand inhabitants – remember Salt Lake City has less than twenty thousand – possesses so fine a theatrical structure. It ranks, alike in capacity, and elegance of structure and finish, along with the opera houses and academies of music of Boston, New York, Philadelphia, Chicago and Cincinnati." Leonard J. Arrington, *Great Basin Kingdom: An Economic History of the Latter-day Saints, 1830-1900* (Urbana, IL: University of Illinois Press, 2004), 211.

supplementary to the curriculum, the arts are treated as a foundational discipline, thanks to a unique public-private partnership in the state.

The Beverly Taylor Sorenson Arts Learning Program – named for the renowned arts education advocate – is dedicated to providing arts funding in local schools. Sorenson spent years successfully working to convince the Utah Legislature to increase funding for arts education, a model appropriately lauded across the state today.

Many conservative states are quick to cut funding for the arts, but Utahns continue to show they value the importance of the creative mind. While government cannot be all things to all people, Utahns have made the arts a top priority.

THE DL 832 RULE

Utah's political community is small. Don't be surprised when you keep running into the same people.

If you take the Delta Monday morning flight (DL 832) to Reagan-National Airport in Washington D.C. you will likely be surrounded by various members of the Utah and Idaho congressional delegations.[74]

On that same flight, you will frequently see influential Utah lobbyists who have work to accomplish in the nation's capital. If you are on this flight and people recognize you, you have officially arrived. Where you have arrived is still in question. It's a fine line between swamp and success.

---

[74] Orrin Hatch said it was on these flights where he would write much of his music. To get the full DL 832 experience, I highly recommend grabbing a Caffeine Free Diet Coke and relaxing to old Hatch songs. My personal favorites include, "It's Not So Easy Growing Old" (stay close to the tissues) and "America Rocks!" as performed by the Osmonds (second generation). The best lyrics of the entire song go as follows, "America rocks! From its busy bustling cities to its quiet country walks, America rocks! It's totally cool, it's totally hot, I mean it's like right there at the top, America rocks!"

THE RAMPTON RURAL TOUR

Get out of the political bubble.

Former Utah Governor Cal Rampton won broad acclaim for his frequent tours to rural Utah. He made it a point to visit areas of the state that were underserved and unable to attend political gatherings in Salt Lake City. In a popular move, Rampton and his wife[75] also spent the night in the home of a local member of the community instead of a nearby hotel. For years to come, rural Utahns would brag to their friends about the night that the governor of Utah spent in their home.[76]

Too often politicians meet with the same people over and over again during the course of their elected terms. Part of this problem comes from a scheduling reality. Most people end up spending the most time with those who consistently request meetings. Don't fall into this trap. It is also important to find ways to spend time in places where people disagree with you. Utahns will respect your willingness to go places where you might not feel welcome. Follow Governor Rampton's example and get out of your own political bubble.

---

[75] Rampton met his wife on a blind date at a 1937 Halloween party. He dressed up as Adolf Hitler (several years before the onset of World War II). His date and soon-to-be wife Lucybeth dressed up as a Russian peasant. She would become the legal secretary for Ernest Wilkinson, future president of BYU and Republican candidate in the 1964 U.S. Senate race against Democrat Frank Moss.

[76] Don't be surprised if voters save forever that voicemail or text that you sent them years ago. I remember receiving a LinkedIn request from Lieutenant Governor Greg Bell, who months before had left his position to return to the private sector. I was ecstatic that someone as important as the lieutenant governor had recognized a relatively anonymous person like me. In my excitement, I immediately fired off a text to share the news with my best friend Spencer Cox, the state's new lieutenant governor. This didn't seem strange to me at the time. No matter how long you have been in office, don't forget how it feels for everyday Utahns to interact with you in the smallest of ways. It creates a remarkably memorable experience that they won't soon forget.

THE GRANATO'S LUNCH SPECIAL

Don't hide behind your staff. Go out and meet with the public.

One of the most popular destinations for Utah politicos has always been Granato's, a local Italian deli owned by former Salt Lake County Councilmember Sam Granato. On any given day, you could find Utahns from all walks of life at the deli, including some of Utah's most prominent elected leaders.

It didn't matter who you were or what your persuasion of politics happened to be, Granato always treated you like family. In 2018, Republicans from across the state joined in mourning the loss of the Democrat Granato, one of the state's finest bridge builders.

As an elected leader, look around at the people with whom you discuss issues that you encounter. If the answer is only individuals who also happen to be on your payroll, then you probably need to expand your circle beyond just your trusted confidantes.[77] Take a trip to Granato's to get a feel for what others might be thinking.[78] You'll be a better public servant as you frequently take the pulse of everyday Utahns.

---

[77] Also a tip for aspiring political staffers. Avoid any self-aggrandizing profile pieces in the media or other opportunities to make yourself the center of attention.

[78] It is of course possible to be too available to the point of being taken for granted by others. Overexposure can be a real concern for some Utahns, especially those prone to excessive media attention.

THE KITTY DUNN RULE

Most of a campaign's work is done by a small number of people.

One of Utah's most brilliant grassroots organizers, Kitty Dunn, has managed campaigns of all varieties throughout the state. Much of the success of Senator Orrin Hatch's convincing 2012 election can be attributed to her leadership.

As with any organization, the work that is accomplished in a political campaign is thanks to a very small number of individuals.[79] It is critical that you identify these people early in the campaign, in order to maximize your grassroots success.[80] Lawn signs don't put themselves up. Doors need to be knocked. Phone calls must be made.[81] In fact, much of what constitutes a successful campaign is rather mundane in nature.[82]

Ironically, most campaigns surround themselves with an inner circle of advisers who do very little of the actual work conducted by a campaign. A good rule of thumb is this: the people who are there with you setting up and taking down your convention booth are your most important team members. They are the people who are the backbone of any good campaign. Divest yourself of the rest and devote your time to people who will actually make the difference in your race.[83]

---

[79] Malcolm Gladwell referred to this as the Law of the Few in his bestseller *The Tipping Point*. "A tiny percentage of people do the majority of the work."
[80] Utah National Guard Adjutant General Jefferson Burton once said about his decision to promote Brigadier General Val Peterson (a Utah Valley University vice president and member of the Utah House of Representatives), "My mantra is if you want something done right, ask a busy guy to do it."
[81] Word to the wise, avoid the Monday night robocall.
[82] One Utahn who got his start in politics through these grassroots efforts was Karl Rove, a student at Olympus High School and future advisor to President George W. Bush.
[83] This is the unspoken secret of the caucus-convention system. While delegates no longer control access to the ballot, their willingness to engage in the political process far more than anyone else assures them a permanent place at the decision-making table.

THE PLUTO PLATTER RULE

Your first idea often won't be your best. Don't be afraid to let someone improve it.

Many Utahns are probably unaware that the inventor[84] of the Frisbee was one of our own, Walter Frederick Morrison from Richfield, Utah.[85] He had the idea after throwing cake pans back and forth with his wife and began producing the product in 1948, selling them at local county fairs.

At first, he named the new product the "Flyin' Cake Pan." With a new design he rebranded it the "Whirlo-Way" and "Flyin' Saucer" before finally settling on "Pluto Platter."

He would later sell the rights to his creation in 1957, and the company changed the name to Frisbee after a northeast bakery where college students liked to toss cake pans. With the new name change, total sales today now exceed 200 million.[86]

In politics, pride of authorship has ruined many a proposal. While your idea may be brilliant, don't be afraid to let others help you in other areas where perhaps you are not so strong.[87]

---

[84] Utah has a proud history of successful inventors besides Morrison. For many years, Philo T. Farnsworth, the inventor of the television, was one of two statues placed in the U.S. Capitol representing Utah. Lester Wire invented the electric traffic light (his day job was as a Salt Lake City police detective). Even the inventor of the Zamboni (Frank Zamboni) is a native of Utah's own Eureka.

[85] Richfield also is the hometown of Joseph Hanson, the right-hand man of Russian revolutionary Leon Trotsky

[86] In another Utah political connection, Utah Representative Kay McIff was Morrison's attorney in the royalties case for the invention.

[87] A state that is home to Stephen Covey could certainly teach you a little thing about teamwork and the value of synergy.

THE JAKE GARN RETIREMENT STRATEGY

Stepping away from the fight on top is the best way to go.

One of the unspoken rules of politics for incumbents is to always tell people you plan to run for reelection. Any doubt on the subject only invites potential challengers. If you decide later you don't want to run, you can always back out. However, once you say you're out, it's nearly impossible to get back in.[88]

And then you have Jake Garn. Perhaps no other Utah politician had such an on-again-off-again relationship with his own retirement.[89]

He went back and forth several times before eventually deciding to run for a third term. He did the same when it came time to run for a fourth term. Eventually he chose to retire, one of only a handful of U.S. Senators from the state to do so voluntarily. His quote when he announced his retirement perhaps best encapsulates his difficult decision:

"I have battled with Jake Garn the Senator, who would love to continue to serve, and Jake Garn the father and husband, who wants to spend more time with his family. Jake Garn the family man won the battle."[90]

Inevitably, people remember you the most for how you leave, not necessarily what you do while in office. Learn the Jake Garn Retirement Strategy and understand when it's time to call it a day. Leaving on top is always the best way to go.

---

[88] Many experts credit former Governor Olene Walker's delayed decision to run as the main cause of her defeat during the 2004 gubernatorial election.

[89] One exception is perhaps Nolan Karras. At a roast of the outgoing Utah House Speaker, KUTV reporter Rod Decker quipped, "The reason Nolan is so good at retiring is he's practiced a lot."

[90] For those who might cynically question Senator Garn's desire to spend more time with his family, don't forget the time Garn donated a kidney to his daughter while serving as a U.S. Senator.

THE HAVEN BARLOW PRINCIPLE

Institutional memory is the foundation of a high-functioning government.

It is quite common for candidates to rail against "career politicians," but seldom do you hear a candidate extol the virtues and immense value created by institutional memory in governmental service.

I wish more of them had a chance to meet former State Senator Haven Barlow, the longest serving legislator in Utah state history. Elected at age 29, Barlow would go on to serve 42 years in both the House and Senate, including six years as Senate President. Many of the key reasons we celebrate Utah's success today can be attributed to the decisions made by Barlow and his peers during those 42 years of service.

Barlow was key in the efforts to make Weber State University a four-year university and the development of numerous applied technology centers across the state. His philanthropic generosity was legendary with one United Way leader saying that Barlow always had "yes in his heart." In his unprecedented legislative and community service he didn't always leave his fingerprints, but his influence is undeniable.[91]

Rather than criticizing elected officials for their length of service, a new member of the city council or legislature would be wise to seek out their counsel. Better yet, find an excuse to meet with your predecessors to learn from them as much as possible. More often than not, that brilliant idea you have today has been tried before. Understanding where your predecessors succeeded or fell short is critical in pushing forward your own efforts in the future.

---

[91] Barlow's son Stewart continues the family tradition as he admirably serves as a respected member of the Utah House of Representatives.

THE FLUORIDATION RULE

Always be clear. Avoid double negatives.

In an effort to improve public health, several communities in the state began pursuing fluoridation during the 1970s, only to be beat back time and time again by referendum efforts. In many instances, the vote wasn't close, even defeating the measure in Utah's largest county (Salt Lake).

Anti-fluoridation citizens went even further in 1976, pushing for a statewide initiative that would prevent the state's health department from implementing a fluoridation mandate statewide. Most politicos expected the initiative to pass relatively easily, as the measure only prohibited statewide implementation but still allowed for local decision-making on the fluoridation issue.

But the way the issue was framed on the ballot confused many voters. A yes vote meant you opposed statewide fluoridation, and a no vote meant you were for it.[92]

Confused voters called their local health departments in droves in hopes of better understanding the initiative. Ultimately, the effort passed in a narrow 52-48 percent vote, although political experts credited voter confusion for a wide swing in the outcome of the race.

The simpler your message in an election, the better.[93] Any small nuance can lead to dramatic swings at the ballot box.

---

[92] See the Judicial Retention Corollary (p. 93).
[93] Proponents of a 2018 statewide ballot question to increase taxes for public education learned this lesson the hard way. Instead of raising funds through traditional measures, the initiative called for a confusing increase in the gas tax.

THE SOCK THEORY

Be approachable. Give people a reason to talk to you.

Nearly every profile piece on Utah Congressman John Curtis includes a reference to his prolific collection of socks, more than 300 pairs in all at last count. Prominent visitors to his office get a pair of crazy-patterned socks on the way out. For a small donation, campaign supporters could receive a pair of specialty John Curtis for Congress socks. He even has his own Pinterest board called "Curtis Socks."

The best part about the socks is that it gives people something to talk about with the Congressman, essentially an ice-breaking moment that makes him immediately approachable. Often in politics, people just need an excuse to talk to prominent political figures. Congressman Curtis took care of that problem for them.

In addition, Curtis teaches the lesson that it's important not only to be approachable in person but also online. He responds quickly to constituents and without much of the formality often seen by prominent political figures. Experts from across the state agree that Curtis is one of Utah's most effective communicators.

Learn the Sock Theory from John Curtis. Being approachable is a must if you want to succeed in Utah politics.

THE J. GOLDEN KIMBALL RULE

A little good-hearted swearing is allowed in Utah politics.

Despite his death in 1938, stories about former LDS leader J. Golden Kimball continue to abound through Utah nearly a century later. Many of these stories appear to be poorly documented folklore – some historians question whether they ever really occurred – and yet they continue to be shared. Perhaps this fact says more about us than it does him.

Kimball credited his growing up on a ranch near Bear Lake[94] for his lifelong penchant for swearing, including during prominent church meetings.[95] He developed the habit as a young man, "You can't drive mules if you can't swear. It's the only language they understand."[96]

We tell and retell the stories of one of Utah's most unique personalities, in large part because his irreverence had a way of cutting to the heart of an issue.

In politics, a little swearing is allowed in the predominantly Mormon state. It demonstrates a no-nonsense approach that many Utahns continue to appreciate.

---

[94] For non-Utahns who find themselves in northern Utah in late summer, don't miss the world famous Bear Lake raspberry shakes. Despite the many places where you can buy the famous desserts, the best raspberry shake in town can be found at the local Chevron convenience store. Trust me.

[95] In his defense, this was probably back when three-hour church was still a thing.*

*If you think three-hour church is bad, just ask former Utah Jazz player Trey Lyles about three-hour basketball practice.

[96] Pat Bagley, "Living History: Mormon 'apostle' shoots mouth off, gun carriers shut up." *Salt Lake Tribune*, 28 December 2012.

THE WILD HORSE THEORY

Words mean different things inside and outside the state.

To a rancher in rural Utah, the words "wild horse" mean a nuisance animal that destroys the west desert rangeland that ultimately determines their livelihood. To someone from outside the state, the words "wild horse" conjures an image of majestic freedom only experienced in the great expanses of the American West.[97] When Utah ranchers talk about the problem of wild horses, they sound heartless to outsiders.[98]

Similarly, in Utah the words "public lands" are frequently connected to ideas of excessive red tape and burdensome government regulations on two-thirds of the state's lands. But to anyone outside the state, the words "public lands" are understood to be the state's pristine national parks that attract visitors from around the globe.[99]

We use the same words, but somehow we mean completely different things.[100] We're talking past each other.

In any political campaign, the issue of branding is critical. The person who defines an idea first, often sets the terms of the debate.[101] When it comes to contentious issues, try to find new ways to describe problems in order to avoid falling into the tiresome trench warfare of modern politics.

---

[97] I think this is also the basic plot of the Disney movie, *Spirit*.

[98] Voted Best Typo of 1991, a July 14 *Deseret News* story reported, "But in the Uintah Basin, most of the wild horses are descended from 20th-century sheepherders, and the genetic blend makes them undesirable."

[99] Much of the state's long-held distrust of the federal government can be attributed to the lack of control Utah leaders feel over much of the state's territory. Conversely, many residents consider the easy access to public lands to be one of the key reasons why they choose to live here. The tension between these two deeply-held beliefs is frequently palpable.

[100] In a fictional book written by KUTV journalist Rod Decker, a local politician says, "When our pioneer forefathers came to this land, they vowed to make the desert blossom as a rose." Decker responds by saying, "Every time they say that, they do something ugly."

[101] Think of the debate on the estate tax (Democrats) versus the death tax (Republicans).

THE SUNDAY CLOSING RULE

Sometimes a court decision is needed to put a policy issue to rest.

For decades, one of Utah's perennial political issues was legislation requiring businesses to close on Sundays. Republican Governor George Clyde vetoed the measure during the 1959 legislative session, but the issue kept coming back.

Another Sunday closing bill passed the 1967 Legislature, only to be vetoed by Democratic Governor Cal Rampton. Rampton's veto came despite numerous personal calls from prominent Utahns, including LDS general authorities encouraging him to sign the bill.[102]

In his explanation for a veto, Rampton mentioned specific constitutional concerns with the legislation. Proponents of the measure saw an opportunity to box in Rampton with another bill that again called for Sunday closures, while addressing each of the governor's concerns. Still uneasy of the proposed bill, Rampton allowed it to become law without his signature. Soon thereafter, the issue would end up in the Utah Supreme Court only to be struck down as unconstitutional in a unanimous decision.

Some issues are so controversial than no amount of legislative negotiation will satisfy parties. The finality of a court decision is sometimes needed before people are willing to move on.[103]

---

[102] Rampton recorded his experience as follows: "The LDS Church, of course, wanted me to sign the bill. Ordinarily the church leaders left me pretty much alone, but on this particular bill I received a number of calls from church leaders of all ranks, including general authorities, urging me to sign it." See the Prohibition Rule (p. 202).

[103] The controversial S.B. 54 is perhaps the most analogous modern example. When certain groups are so opposed to each other, there isn't much room for negotiation.

INTERMISSION

Stop whatever you are doing. This may be the most important section of the book. If you are expecting a child or have a grandchild on the way, consider these critical rules before giving them a name, especially if you think they just might become the future governor of Utah.

Giving your child the right name will never guarantee their political success, but you can certainly make it easier on them in case they ever decide to run.

THE LILJENQUIST RULE

If possible, avoid using a long and hard to pronounce name.

This rule gets its name from former Utah State Senator Dan Liljenquist, who unsuccessfully challenged U.S. Senator Orrin Hatch in the 2012 Republican primary.

The rule breaks down in two separate ways:

- Length – As a general rule, the longer the name the worse it is in politics. This is true in Utah and across the country with very few exceptions. The biggest exception to this would be someone with a very prominent, well-known name (e.g. Kennedy or Huntsman).
- Hard to Pronounce – If someone has a hard to pronounce name, chances are people won't remember you. Any time a news publication puts a pronunciation guide after your name, you know it's problematic. In fact, a 2011 study in the *Journal of Experimental Social Psychology* concluded that the easier it is to pronounce a person's name, the more likely you are to vote for them.

Liljenquist was smart and fixed the problem by putting on all campaign signs his first name is large bold print, "DAN" and a much smaller "Liljenquist" below.

Sometimes this can't be resolved. But usually one of your names works better than the other. Almost always it's the shorter one.

THE AIMEE WINDER NEWTON COROLLARY

Don't be afraid to emphasize certain parts of your name.

I recently read a book titled *Utah in the Year 2050*, written by Representative Mike Winder,[1] sibling of Salt Lake County Councilmember Aimee Winder Newton.[2] In the acknowledgement section, he thanks his sibling, "Aimee Newton."

Maybe by the year 2050 she will return to this name, but to almost all Utahns she is known as "Aimee Winder Newton" not "Aimee Newton." Prior to running for public office, Newton wisely decided to include her maiden name to remind voters of her connection to the prominent Utah family.

Sometimes it may be your maiden name. Other times it may be a seldom-used middle name, but it's acceptable in politics to emphasize a different part of your name.

In a similar vein, you can slightly change your name to make it more appealing. For example, former President Jimmy Carter's real name was James Earl Carter, but he went by the more folksy Jimmy, a name that would show up on ballots across America. William Jefferson Clinton went by the simpler name "Bill," when he ran for public office. And locally, GOP legend Richard Richards went by the much shorter first name "Dick" for obvious reasons.[3] In politics, it's okay to emphasize certain parts of your name more than others.

---

[1] Winder is one of Utah's most prolific writers with other important books such as *Presidents & Prophets: The Story of America's Presidents and the LDS Church*.

[2] Newton is one of the rising stars in Utah politics. I expect future chapters to be written about her in the years ahead.

[3] Richards was one of the most successful GOP party leaders, serving as National Republican Committee chairman and a close confidante of President Ronald Reagan. Richards helped organized the former president's trip to the state, introducing him to crowds in Hooper and Ogden.

THE JONATHAN JOHNSON III COROLLARY

Never use Roman numerals in your name.[4]

In the 2016 gubernatorial primary, Republican Jonathan Johnson ran against incumbent Governor Gary Herbert.

Johnson wisely changed the way he publicly presented himself in anticipation of his gubernatorial run. He had previously gone by the name Jonathan Johnson III, but for the campaign went by the simpler Jonathan Johnson.

Whenever someone sees a Roman numeral after your name, they assume you own a sailboat. Owning a sailboat is never a good thing in politics.

---

[4] A much better alternative is giving your child the title "Jr." Jon Huntsman Jr. sounds far better than Jon Huntsman II. In an interesting case study on this issue, famous NBA star Gary Payton actually named two of his children "Gary," one Gary Payton II and the other Gary Payton Jr. Gary Payton II starred on Salt Lake Community College's basketball team and would later sign with the Los Angeles Lakers.

THE LAVAUN THEORY

Certain names you immediately know are from Utah.

If you have lived in the state long enough, there are certain names you hear that immediately remind you of Utah. My grandfather was named LaVaun Cox,[5] a name that virtually anyone in the state would recognize as local. LaVarr is another easy tell.

Some of these names could come from references with the LDS Church's Book of Mormon. Think Nephi, Jacob, Jarom, and Teancum. Some might come from modern-day church leaders, including Brigham or Kimball.

Other times (and especially in recent years), Utahns have chosen unique combination names (e.g. Kambree, Taylyn and Kynlee) or creatively spelled names (my youngest sister is named Caytee). Bonus points are given if you can include multiple capital letters in the same name (LaVell and LeRoy).

If you want to make sure voters know your child is from Utah, giving them a unique name is always a good start. But let's do our best to not get too carried away.

---

[5] Cox also served as Utah Senate Majority Leader as a Democrat. One of my favorite quotes from my grandpa comes from a *Deseret News* profile piece about his friend Republican Congressman Howard Nielson.* He was quoted in the article as saying, "Howard's not a bit colorful, and he has a low humor quotient, but he's smart as hell." Ken Perkins, "2 Demos Vying for Chance to Unseat Nielson." *Deseret News*, 22 June 1988.
*Nielson also served as a member of the Utah Legislature. As a member of the minority party in the early 1970s, he was tasked with the responsibility of coming up with a redistricting plan for the body. His proposal was accepted with only minor tweaks by the Democratic majority.

THE V. LOWRY SNOW RULE

It's common for Utah candidates (and Latter-day Saint general authorities) to go by their middle names.

This rule is named for Representative V. Lowry Snow who goes by his middle name, and of all politicians in the state strikes me as the one most similar to an LDS general authority.[6]

I believe there is no other state in the nation that has such a significant number of influential leaders who go by their middle names. Some members of the church even joke about this middle-name propensity among so many church leaders.

The extra formality of an initial can add a degree of gravitas. In general, the rule on when to use first initials in politics is yes for letters and stationary, but no for campaign signs.

The one exception to this rule is if a candidate goes by their middle name and has a first name beginning with the letter, "C." In this case, the gravitas given to the name is lost by the confusing nature of the name. Just ditch the initial altogether and stick with your middle name. A prime example of this is former LDS general authority and a current state senator in southern Idaho, C. Scott Grow. Inevitably, any name that begins with a "C." followed by a name sounds like the title of a children's book.[7]

---

[6] As a freshman legislator, I remember attending a meeting with Representative Snow. It wasn't an issue of much importance, but I remember aggressively making my case to the various parties in attendance. I am eternally grateful he had patience with an overconfident young legislator like myself who still had so much to learn.
[7] I've thought a lot about this since my name is technically C. Jon Cox. I also respond to C. Jon Run and C. Jon Jump.

THE MIA LOVE MODEL

Simple, easy to remember names are always the best.

If you want your child to have a political future in the state of Utah, consider the name Mia Love. Technically, her first given name is Ludmya and Love is her married name, so Mia deserves just as much credit for the name as her parents.

The beauty of the name is that it works well with either the first or last name alone, but it also sounds great together. It's easy to pronounce and yet fresh and unique at the same time.

Parents take note. Hands down, Mia Love has the best name in Utah politics.

THE REAGAN NAME DILEMMA

Any parent who names their child "Reagan," will definitely run for political office at least once in their lives.

Naming your child, "Reagan," says more about you as the parents than it does your child.

I know of several elected officials in Utah who have named their child after former President Ronald Reagan.[8] I remember one recent candidate for Congress mentioning this prominently on their campaign website.

Also, if you're spending significant amounts of time worrying about your unborn child's political career, you have problems and need to immediately seek help.

---

[8] The hit television show *30 Rock* refers to the principle of "Reaganing," as a complete 24-hour period of time when a person doesn't make a single mistake. U.S. Senator Orrin Hatch even makes a brief cameo on the show (Season 2: Episode 2).

THE ABE LINCOLN JENKINS RULE

If all else fails, make up a name.[9]

Technically, you don't have to use your real name when you run for public office. The county clerk won't check your birth certificate,[10] as a 2018 candidate for U.S. Senate in Utah recently found out. Despite a legal name of Brian Jenkins, the Utah man filed to run as Abe Lincoln Brian Jenkins in his official candidate filing. He even dressed up as the former president in his various appearances across the state.

After being defeated in the GOP convention, the good-natured Jenkins also appeared in various commercials encouraging increased voter turnout for the state's residents.

---

[9] Another Utahn who made use of this rule, albeit for reasons other than politics was Robert Leroy Parker, better known as the infamous Butch Cassidy. As a random aside, Cassidy also happened to be a distant cousin to Utah Governor Gary Herbert. Herbert commented that his grandfather remembered knowing Cassidy, saying once to the family, "I knew Butch Cassidy. He's nothing but a darn crook."

[10] This seems like a real missed opportunity for a conspiracy theory with the birther crowd.

CHAPTER 4

THE MEDIA

THE WORKING THE REFS RULE

If you feel mistreated by the media, let them know but don't expect the story to change.

From time to time, you may feel mistreated by the local news media. As an elected official or candidate, you may want to lash out publicly about this perceived mistreatment. Avoid it in all but the most egregious examples. You will come across as whiny to the public, and if anything the media member will only double down on the story.

Complaining about not getting coverage won't encourage members of the media to start covering your struggling campaign. Publicly whining about the slant of that coverage will seldom lead to any improvements.

A better approach is to express to the member of the media your concerns, along with the reasons why you disagree. You shouldn't expect a retraction or correction of the piece, but most media members will take the criticism to heart.

We call this rule "working the refs" because similar to a sports event,[1] a coach or player will complain to referees throughout the game but almost

---

[1] As a politician, it's best to avoid speaking or being recognized at a sporting event. The probability for booing is a little too high, either from political opponents or more likely fans of the losing team who are mad at everything at that moment.

never will it cause the official to change the call after the fact. If the complaint never works, why continue such an unproductive strategy? The key is the next call.[2]

Remember in politics, it's all about the long game. It takes thick skin to live life "under the gun and above the fold." If you can't handle the pressure, politics might not be the place for you.[3]

---

[2] The Bill Smart Corollary to this rule is that escalating your complaint to an editor almost always makes it worse. Smart was the former editor and general manager of the *Deseret News*. Longtime political reporter LaVarr Webb wrote a column angering Governor Scott Matheson who called Smart to complain. The governor was so upset that he demanded an in-person meeting with the paper's executives and Webb, who recounted the meeting as follows, "I listened with trepidation as the state's most powerful person outlined why he thought my column was unfair and one-sided and questioned whether I could be an objective reporter. Bill gently but firmly reminded the governor that the column was an opinion piece and fell within the realm of fair criticism of a public official. He defended my judgment and ability to both report objectively and write an opinion column."

[3] Named after the prominent former reporter, the Glen Warchol Rule of Utah politics is a reminder that journalists believe it is a key part of their job description to challenge those in positions of authority. Colleague Robert Gehrke remarked of Warchol, "On the surface, Glen reveled in being a pain in the ass...He was never as giddy as when he was putting his finger in the eye of powerful people. It was like a challenge to him — and that made him a really excellent reporter."

THE COLTRIN COROLLARY

Consistently criticizing the media never ends well.

Bill Coltrin was a longtime sportswriter for the *Salt Lake Tribune*. One day, legendary coach LaVell Edwards complained to Coltrin about the coverage his team at the time, Granite High School, was receiving. Edwards wanted to set the record straight.

Coltrin told him, "Be careful about how much spouting off you do, even if you're right. They go to press 365 days a year. You'll have your one day in the sun, but they'll have their 365."

If you're ever tempted to take the media to task, remember the Coltrin Corollary.[4] Even in a digital age, the media still buys their ink by the barrel.

---

[4] Unless your name is Donald Trump.

THE CLARIFICATION COROLLARY

The most important news cycle is always the first.

Any time a story includes your name and the word "clarified," you know it's going to be a bad story. Sometimes it's necessary to clarify your previous comments, but often you're just extending a bad news cycle even longer. Focus on getting that first news cycle right, if at all possible.

To illustrate this principle, look at the mystery hijacker, D.B. Cooper. He purchased a plane ticket using the fake name, "Dan Cooper" with no middle name or initial. But in the first news story about the hijacking, the media mistakenly used the name "D.B.," instead of "Dan." Once the mistake had been made and entered the public consciousness, it stuck and never changed.[5]

Similarly, no matter how many times you clarify a previous news report, it's that first news cycle that will stick with people.

---

[5] Mostly I wanted to mention D.B. Cooper so I could share a little-known story in Utah history. Several months after the mystery hijacker made off with $200,000 in the legendary crime, BYU student Richard McCoy did the exact same thing but managed to earn an even higher ransom, $500,000. McCoy hijacked a plane in California and after collecting the ransom parachuted out of the plane over Provo. He was arrested days later and sentenced to 45 years in prison. Several years later, he escaped the maximum security prison in Virginia and was killed in the subsequent manhunt. To this day, some experts believe McCoy may have been the original D.B. Cooper.

THE DOUG WRIGHT TREATMENT

A politician is much more likely to open up to someone they view as a friend.

For decades, the most high-profile interviews in the state would go to KSL radio legend Doug Wright.[6] If a politician was in the middle of a scandal, they wouldn't go on any program, except for the Doug Wright Show.

The reason was simple. Wright would let them talk uninterrupted to give their side of the story. At times, some insiders wanted Wright to punch back. However, there's a reason why people kept coming back on the program. They knew that no matter what, they would be given a fair chance to make their case.[7]

I recently participated in my neighborhood caucus with only a few other people in attendance, including Doug and his wife. When we discussed a particularly bitter race, I expressed my disgust with one of the candidates who I disliked. The rest of our precinct asked for Wright's opinion of the same candidate. Instead of blasting him, Wright said, "Now, he would make an excellent neighbor – the kind of person you would want to invite over for a barbecue – but I don't think he's the best person in this race."

It's not a show. At his core, he's a legitimately kind individual who wants to give people the benefit of the doubt.

---

[6] Wright's daily presence on KSL was a mainstay for a generation of Utahns. While he continues to participate with the station in a variety of ways, his show is noticeably missed by Utahns from across the entire political spectrum.

[7] For those critical of Wright's interview style, remember that some of the biggest campaign blunders have occurred in a non-confrontational interview format. Thinking you're among friends often leads to a politician letting their guard down.

DECKERING

*Even in a genteel state like Utah, politicians should not expect to escape
tough questions from the media.*

Growing up, I remember watching the nightly news and always seeing
KUTV reporter and Utah journalism's patron saint Rod Decker. At the
time, I thought he seemed so aggressive and even a little abrasive. Maybe it
was the tone of his voice. Maybe it was his volume. Or possibly it was
simply the way he seemed to badger some of Utah's most prominent
political figures.

In many ways, Deckering is the polar opposite of the Doug Wright
Treatment. And yet, both are effective in the Beehive State. One of them
opens you up by showering you with praise and allowing you as much
time as you want to respond. Deckering is very different. He peppers you
with in-your-face questions, sometimes interrupting your answers if
necessary. But to Decker's credit, he never plays "gotcha" and never
purposely tries to make you look foolish (although some politicians
manage to do that all on their own). He also happens to be incredibly
likeable with a one-of-a-kind personality that will be sorely missed in Utah
journalism.

Both men are legends for completely different reasons and often to
completely different audiences. If you want to make a difference in Utah,
remember Rod Decker. Sometimes the most memorable Utahns are
completely different than the norm.[8]

---

[8] Do yourself a favor and go read one of Rod Decker's books. He really is a Utah treasure. My
favorite Amazon review of his fictional book, *Environment for Murder*, goes as follows:
"Having grown up in Utah and enjoying Mr. Decker's other work as a TV reporter, I have
enjoyed this book a great deal. He's not afraid to expose all of the nuances of the local politics
and religion. I laughed a lot! Only in Utah can you picture the main character driving to
Sunday dinner across town, nursing a hangover, smoking four cigarettes along the way. Then
he's greeted by his nephews playing basketball in their Sunday clothes, and the aroma of
overcooked roast beef."

THE KUED RULE

If you want to influence public policy, you must understand the rhythm and flow of the news cycle.

For years, Utah governors have appeared on the governor's monthly news conference on KUED. Any member of the media is welcome to ask the governor any question at the event. No question is off limits.

As a staff member for Governor Gary Herbert, we would try to anticipate what questions a reporter might ask. Reporters are often already writing stories on another item of interest that day and consequently looking for quotes to plug into their piece. During a legislative session, this is easy. Look through the legislative hearings scheduled that day or the floor calendar and you are almost guaranteed to know what kinds of questions you will be asked.

I would often chuckle about legislators who were furious about a headline that showed up when the governor weighed in on their bill. They felt like we had gone out of our way to comment on it, as if we had held a special press conference just for that one comment. In reality, their bill just happened to have a hearing as the same day as the governor's press availability and the reporter was looking to fill a quote.[9]

If you want the press to cover your story, know when they have their own internal meetings to pitch potential stories for the day. Get to know your local reporter. Spend some time with the editorial board. Every news medium is a little different, and their own rhythms and flows are not all the same. The sooner you understand how they work, the more likely you are to be successful in communicating with the public.

---

[9] Here's a little trick for legislators, interest groups, and other Utahns engaged in the public policy process. If you want a public official to take a position on an issue important to you, hold a media event the same day that official has press availability.

THE SHELBY COROLLARY

Beware of press releases issued late on a Friday afternoon.

Late on a Friday afternoon only a few days before Christmas 2013, Judge Robert Shelby shocked the state by announcing his decision that the constitutional amendment banning gay marriage in Utah would be overturned.

This was by far the biggest news story of the year, but no one was ready for the announcement. To make matters even more complicated, many reporters and government officials were out of the office getting ready to celebrate the Christmas holiday.

Usually a Friday afternoon news story is an opportunity for a person to convey an unpopular news item in a way that will receive the least amount of public attention. The communications professional thinks they are being so clever, but the media understands exactly what they are hoping to accomplish.

Interestingly, the same tactic appears to be employed by many courts across the country, albeit for likely different reasons. Perhaps in an effort to depoliticize an issue, it is not uncommon for a court to issue a Friday decision late in the day.

THE STATE OF THE UNION SEATING RULE

Building a public profile can be exhausting.

An article from the national publication *Politico* stated that because it is open seating for members of Congress during the president's annual State of the Union speech, it takes a member an estimated 13 hours of waiting in a seat on the House floor in order to end up by the aisle (where they could potentially shake the president's hand on live national television). To get both near an aisle and next to Republican leaders would obviously take a lot longer.

The assignment cannot be farmed out to a staffer, the member of Congress must be the one who saves their spot.[10] And yet year after year, one of Utah's congressional members was always there, either on the aisle or right next to his party's leader and in full view of television screens across the country.[11]

The fact that we have members of Congress waiting around for more than 13 hours in order to get on television is undoubtedly a sad reflection of the state of affairs in Washington D.C. But much of the work that goes into creating a public profile is similarly frustrating.

It is possible to succeed in politics without building such a public profile. Instead of camping out in front of television cameras, you can dedicate yourself to your policy work. However, there are political advantages to having the bully pulpit that inevitably come with such a platform. Choose wisely what kind of elected leader you want to be.

---

[10] Consider it the House of Representatives version of filibustering.
[11] Hint: The former congressman's godfather was Sandy Koufax.

THE DAN JONES RULE

Polls are tremendously valuable to a campaign.

One of the greatest minds in the history of Utah politics was longtime pollster Dan Jones.[12] His institutional memory is without equal, thanks in no small part to the decades of polling he has conducted for numerous candidates and businesses throughout the state.[13]

However, very few candidates understand how best to maximize this absolutely critical information. People like to back winners. In many ways, polling numbers can quickly lead to a self-fulfilling prophecy. Smart politicos will understand how best to manage this ever-important expectations game.

The poster child of this brilliant campaign tactic was the 1992 Mike Leavitt gubernatorial race. It was an open seat, with Leavitt trailing other better known candidates. In the days leading up to when polling would be conducted, Leavitt made a strong media push even though the conventional wisdom said a candidate should be focused on delegates.[14]

You see same this strategy frequently employed by broadcast journalists during sweeps month. They will advertise their own programming more, and the stories will be more compelling because the results of sweeps month dictate advertising rates in the months ahead. In investing circles, this principle is referred to as the Keynesian Beauty Contest. As an example of how the principle operates in a fictitious beauty contest, judges are asked two simple questions: (1) what animal do they believe is the cutest, and (2) what animal do they believe other judges will rate as the

---

[12] One of my final edits in this book changed the verb to the past tense "was," due to the recent passing of legendary Utahn Dan Jones. I don't believe we fully comprehend yet what we've lost, the finest mind in a generation of Utah politics.

[13] Jones was the pollster for every Utah governor since Democrat Scott Matheson.

[14] Why waste money so early in the race when clearly it was a delegate war? The answer was simple. Leavitt was playing the long game (as he so often did as governor).

cutest. In test after test, researchers find a wide disparity between the two answers.

Economist John Maynard Keynes, for whom the concept is named, believes this is why such pricing swings can exist in the stock market. Investors frequently buy and sell stocks not because they believe that is their actual value but because they believe other investors perceive them to have that value. Those two ways of decision-making can lead to completely different outcomes. Yet this is exactly what the political class does all the time in elections. You donate your time and your efforts to the candidate you think others will choose to win, regardless of who you believe should win. The same is true with individual voters. Consider this example from the 2000 presidential election:

"In one study, they tracked Democratic and Republican voters before the 2000 U.S. presidential election. When George W. Bush gained in the polls, Republicans rated him as more desirable, but so did Democrats, who were already preparing justifications for the anticipated status quo. The same happened when Al Gore's likelihood of success increased: both Republicans and Democrats judged him more favorably. Regardless of political ideologies, when a candidate seemed destined to win, people liked him more. When his odds dropped, they liked him less."[15]

When the smart money is on a candidate that no one really likes, the crash can be swift and unexpected. On occasion, a candidate is able to prove the polls wrong. But the self-fulfilling prophecy of polls often leads to more support for the candidate expected to win. In the end, politics is not always about who is actually winning and who is losing, or even who we think should win or lose.

Ignore such polls at your own peril.

---

[15] Adam Grant. *Originals: How Non-Conformists Move the* Word (New York: Penguin Books, 2016), 6.

THE TOM BARBERI RULE

Sometimes the polls are wrong.

Always annoyed by the press declaring winners before votes had even been counted, Utah radio legend Tom Barberi[16] conducted an experiment. On Election Day 1984, Barberi encouraged his listeners to lie to exit pollsters in order to make the election results a little more unpredictable. It all started as a joke, but many Barberi listeners took him seriously.

Almost immediately after the polls closed, two local stations announced contradictory results of the state's congressional race between Republican David Monson and Democrat Francis Farley, one calling the race for the Democrat Farley with a comfortable 20-point margin of victory.

Monson ended up winning by the narrowest of margins, 0.2 percent, 496 votes in all. Barberi couldn't have been more pleased with the embarrassment and the blame he received from across the state for the mishap.

Polls can be instructive tools in understanding the electorate, but their usefulness has limits. One-time polling can be especially dangerous. Stick with respected firms to receive the most trustworthy results.

---

[16] Do yourself a favor and buy a copy of his book, *Legalizing Adulthood in Utah*. Always irreverent and insightful, you will enjoy the read. A few of my favorite lines in the book:
-"Where there's smoke, there's probably a city councilman" (p. 15).
-"Few things in life can unnerve a person more than the stark realization that he actually agrees with something that Senator Orrin Hatch said" (p. 5).
-"I don't trust people whose first names are letters" (p. 339).
-"Robert Garff, Speaker of the House in Utah, came out the other day and saw his shadow, indicating 17 more days of silliness up on the hill"(p. 262).

THE BAGLEY TREATMENT

It's better to be criticized than not talked about at all.

This principle of Utah politics gets its name from longtime *Salt Lake Tribune* cartoonist, Pat Bagley. For decades, Bagley has excoriated prominent Utah politicians, especially members of the Republican majority.[17] You know you've finally arrived in Utah politics when you are individually targeted in a Bagley cartoon.

For members of the Legislature, Bagley always draws an identical image, short, balding, double-chinned, and completely forgettable. However, he occasionally draws a unique character, and that is the moment to be celebrated.

The interesting thing is how nearly every politician wears a Bagley cartoon as a badge of honor. Many are framed on their desks, even when they are completely mean-spirited. One recent Utah House Speaker had two copies of the exact same cartoon framed in his office.

Courting an occasional bit of controversy is not necessarily a bad thing, even in relatively mild-mannered Utah.

---

[17] Bagley put together a 2010 calendar mocking the Utah Legislature published by a company called White Horse Books.

THE COLD FUSION PRINCIPLE

You can overdo a marketing push.

Two University of Utah professors took the world by complete surprise in 1989 when they announced they had discovered the secret to cold fusion. The university proudly marketed the exciting news, including a congressional request for $25 million to continue research in the important field. Soon thereafter, other researchers discovered that the results were fictitious, and the university came away from the episode completely embarrassed.

This kind of public relations fiasco is not limited to the sciences. In politics, sometimes politicians are anxious to declare "Mission Accomplished" only to have those same words come back to haunt them years down the road. Don't be afraid to promote the successes of your policy effort, but also recognize areas where you still may fall short.

At all times, make sure the degree that you publicly tout a success is commensurate with its real-world impact.

THE SPENCER HALL RULE

Never engage in an online fight with someone you've never met in person.

As social media has made it easier and easier to communicate remotely with people all across the globe, the lack of in-person communication has also led to an increase in online hostility. The solution offered by former KSL news director Spencer Hall is simple: avoid disagreeing online with someone until you first disagree in person. The immediate result would be a much more civil online dialogue.

We have all seen lengthy fights in online comments or on Facebook. Inevitably, no hearts are changed and the increasingly angry discourse only serves to distance the public from wanting to engage in politics.

If you're tempted to start slinging mud online, remember the Spencer Hall Rule and first sit down face to face with your potential adversary.[18]

---

[18] I never learned this rule with prominent politico (and prolific writer) Connor Boyack. Lunch is on me, Connor.

CHAPTER 5

UNDER FIRE

THE DOUGLAS STRINGFELLOW THEORY

Utahns are willing to forgive many things. Blatant lying isn't one of them.

Douglas Stringfellow was elected to Congress and quickly became one of Utah's most popular politicians, with frequent public appearances where he shared his remarkable experience as a World War II[1] spy stuck behind German enemy lines. Utah audiences marveled at the story of him parachuting in the dark of night and a heroic attempt to capture German atomic scientist Otto Hahn, only to be apprehended by the Gestapo. His miraculous escape from a concentration camp made the story even more astonishing.

Except that none of it was true.

Stringfellow only spent two weeks in France as a private before being injured by a landmine, an incident that would partially disable the future congressman. Returning home to Utah for months of medical treatment, Stringfellow created a much more interesting narrative for his injury and war history. The lie spiraled out of control in the years ahead, but not before Stringfellow won a landslide election to Congress. He gave hundreds of speeches across the state and country and even signed a contract for his life's story to be portrayed in a blockbuster movie.

---

[1] The conclusion World War II has a Utah connection as the Enola Gay crew that dropped the world's first atomic bomb on Hiroshima trained at the Wendover Airfield.

When the lie began to unravel, Stringfellow was confronted by Utah Senators Wallace Bennett, Arthur Watkins and LDS Church President David O. McKay. Eventually confessing to the lie, Stringfellow dropped out of his reelection race just days before the election. Unemployable and rejected by Utahns, Stringfellow moved to Mexico never to return again.

Once you lose credibility as a candidate, you have nothing left. Guard your reputation zealously and avoid even the smallest of lies.

In other Utah circles, we sometimes refer to the Doug Stringfellow Theory as "Derek Fishering."[2] When you think of all the former players for the Utah Jazz, why is Fisher so detested? Plenty of players have left, and angry Jazz fans may have lashed out at the player in the moment. But the anger never seems to stick.[3] If a player says something negative about the state or its fans, Jazz fans might get stirred up, but over time the anger dissipates.

But not with Derek Fisher.

Not only did he lie to us, but his lies played with our emotions along the way. When he returned for his dramatic entrance in the 2007 playoffs, we all cried. We celebrated his success, and we all wished him and his family the very best. And then his carefully crafted narrative came crashing down, which helps explain why the anger has such permanence.[4]

In Utah, we can tolerate a lot of bad behavior. We believe in second chances. But don't lie to us. The short-term benefits are never worth the long-term price you almost always end up paying.

---

[2] This section of the book is brought to you by our friend and famous Twitter personality Jimbo Slice. For those who still believe Derek Fisher's narrative, I would suggest you go talk to the Dallas Mavericks.

[3] Of course, I am eternally petty and insist on eating at Zupas every time the Boston Celtics come to town.

[4] The official reason for his contract being voided was the need to access out-of-state medical care for his young daughter.

THE DRIVING HOME TEST

Stick to your convictions, no matter the political pressure.

In U.S. Senator Bob Bennett's farewell address to the U.S. Senate, he shared this advice given to him by his colleague Orrin Hatch.

"Senator Hatch gave me this piece of advice. We were talking one night about an issue, and we were on opposite sides. That didn't happen very often. Senator Hatch and I don't confer in advance of a vote very often. We come to our own conclusions, but, both being conservative Republicans, we usually end up in the same place. On this occasion, we were different. Orrin was giving me his full court press. You have all been exposed to Orrin's full court press on an issue [laughter]. Finally, he said to me: Bob, apply the driving home test. I said: All right, what is the driving home test? He said: After this is all over and the lights go out and you go get in your car and you are driving home, thinking back on the day and the votes you cast, the driving home test is, how will you feel driving home if you cast that particular vote? I said: Orrin, that is some of the best advice I ever got. I voted against him, and I felt great while I was driving home."[5]

With an elected position can come great pressure to bend to the political winds of the day. Resist it and your peers will respect you more than if you had acquiesced to their demands. The earlier you do this in your political service, the better. If others find that you will bend to pressure, you will not only lose their respect but will also guarantee a lot more pressure on your future political decisions.

---

[5] "Sen. Robert Bennett's Farewell Address." *The Hill*, 28 December 2010.

THE MEL BROWN RULE

Time is on your side. Utahns love a good comeback story.

Former Speaker of the House Mel Brown was one of Utah's most powerful politicians, a two-term speaker who planned to run for an unprecedented third term. And then everything came crumbling down.

Marital troubles and an ethics investigation clouded Brown's political future. The now-disgraced politician bowed out of the speaker's race and eventually left the House of Representatives.

Fast forward many years and Brown was again reelected to the House of Representatives, this time in a different district. Starting slowly as a backbencher, Brown eventually saw his opportunity to strike when Representative Becky Lockhart challenged incumbent Speaker Dave Clark. Winning by just one vote,[6] Lockhart promoted Brown to be the powerful House Chair of Executive Appropriations, one of the most important positions in the entire Legislature.[7]

In politics, be patient as time has a way of healing many old wounds. You may be down today, but there is always a tomorrow in Utah politics.[8]

---

[6] See the Karras Thank You Card Rule (p. 62).
[7] As with many comeback stories, Mel Brown again fell from power. In 2014, he ran for the coveted position of Speaker of the House. His loss in the speaker's race was followed by his defeat in the 2016 Republican primary by Logan Wilde, a well-liked sheep and cattle rancher from Morgan County.
[8] Winston Churchill once said, "Politics is almost as exciting as war, and quite as dangerous. In war, you can only be killed once, but in politics, many times."

THE SYRIAN REFUGEE RULE

If done right, you can actually build support by standing up to your own party.[9]

Several years ago, Republican governors across the country began issuing executive orders banning the entrance of Syrian refugees. The legality of such bans was dubious at best, but it didn't stop every Republican governor from issuing the exact same order. Except one.

Utah Governor Gary Herbert is better known for his collaborative personality and desire to work together with parties from all different walks of life. Herbert didn't go along with his peers, and instead issued a statement saying, "Utahns are well known for our compassion for those who are fleeing the violence in their homeland, and we will work to do all we can to ease their suffering without compromising public safety."[10]

And then the phones started to ring. Thousands and thousands of Utah residents called the governor's office[11] to express their outrage that the governor would not stand up for the state's safety. Cable television stations ran around the clock showing maps of the country, with states colored based on where Syrian refugees were still welcome. Only one Republican state made the list: Utah.

After a week, a curious thing began to happen. The phones kept ringing, but the message slowing began to change. What looked like uniform opposition to the stand quickly became mixed responses. Those mixed responses slowly turned to overwhelmingly supportive calls and thank-you letters.

---

[9] A slight variation of this principle on the national level has been called the Sister Souljah Rule.
[10] Matt Canham, "Utah's members of Congress want to halt Syrian refugee program now." *Salt Lake Tribune*, 18 November 2015.
[11] In TV legend Rod Decker's fictional book, *An Environment for Murder*, he tells the story of a local reporter calling the Utah governor's office. The number used in the 1994 book is still the same number used more than 20 years later, (801) 538-1000.

As the governor's spokesman at the time, I remembered going into hiding for a while in hopes of not inflaming the far right any more. I let our initial statement stand, hoping news reporters would move on to a new issue (see the Clarification Corollary, p. 166).

Several days later, KUTV called to say they were doing a story on the LDS Church donating $5 million to aid refugees abroad, including praise from leaders of the church for those countries who were accepting refugees. Would the governor's office be willing to comment on the story? I couldn't say yes fast enough.

Later, the church would come out with additional support for various refugee programs, including mentions in several general conference addresses. From then on, the issue never really came back in any sort of negative way.[12] The State of Utah was not destined to be a leader on refugee issues. We were not destined to lead out on immigration reform with the Utah Compact. That took a lot of hard work and quite a few angry phone calls to get there.

As people engaged in politics, you have the unique ability to change public opinion on an issue. You are not simply there to gauge voter preferences and respond accordingly. Occasionally, you can actually shape it.

---

[12] Soon after the crisis, Herbert responded via Facebook to a proposed Muslim ban in what would become his most viewed social media post ever. He said at the time, "In 1879 under the direction of President Rutherford B. Hayes, the U.S. Secretary of State William Evarts requested that foreign governments no longer allow Mormons to emigrate to the United States in order to prevent the 'large numbers of immigrants [who] come to our shores every year from the various countries of Europe for the avowed purpose of joining the Mormon community at Salt Lake.' Utah exists today because foreign countries refused to grant the wishes of a misguided president and his secretary of state. I am the governor of a state that was settled by religious exiles who withstood persecution after persecution, including an extermination order from another state's governor. In Utah, the First Amendment still matters. That will not change so long as I remain governor."

THE ENID GREENE CRISIS MANAGEMENT THEORY

If a scandal hits, be as transparent as possible as soon as possible.

The nature of the 24-7 news media means that the longer a crisis plays out, the more damage a candidate will suffer. Such immediacy can be terrifying for a candidate or public official, but a lesson can be learned from former member of Congress Enid Greene. When her campaign finance scandal emerged,[13] she immediately held a press conference where she tearfully[14] responded to questions from reporters about the scandal. While most crisis management consultants will advise you to avoid such media attention, Greene did just the opposite.

And not only did she answer reporters' interrogations, she stayed there as long as anyone still had a question. The approximately five-hour press conference must hold a record for politicians, and yet, the excruciating ordeal helped Greene move forward sooner than would have otherwise been possible.

If you have bad news to share,[15] the worst thing that you can do is allow a slow drip of bad news to drag the story out longer than it otherwise would.[16] Get ahead of a news story if you can, and never wait to share bad news.

---

[13] In a little known fact, the grand jury for Greene was convened under the direction of Eric Holder, the future U.S. Attorney General for President Barack Obama.

[14] See the Larry H. Miller Credit Card Theory (p. 129)

[15] Another successful example of admitting a mistake came from U.S. Senator Orrin Hatch, who voted against a bill to designate a federal holiday for Martin Luther King Jr. The Utah Senator subsequently said, "One of the worst decisions I have made as a senator was to vote against making Dr. Martin Luther King's birthday a national holiday...Creating a federal holiday for Martin Luther King was the right thing to do. My vote against it was the wrong choice. I'm grateful I was on the losing side." Orrin Hatch, *Square Peg: Confessions of a Citizen Senator* (New York: Basic Books, 2003), 166-7.

[16] In fact, political adversaries may try to employ such a tactic against you. They won't release the entire binder of opposition research all at once, but instead drop little morsels of damaging information that continues to get media coverage day after day.

THE ALLAN HOWE COROLLARY

Not coming clean with your shortcomings will only make it worse.

In 1976, Congressman Allan Howe ran for reelection against 36-year old political novice Dan Marriott. A few months before the election, Howe was caught in the prostitution sting by two undercover police officers.[17] To make matters worse, his campaign manager was also busted around the same time for selling marijuana to an undercover cop.[18]

Top Democratic leaders called for Howe to step aside, but he refused. The campaign of incumbent U.S. Senator Frank Moss was especially upset with Howe for staying in the race as they believed it harmed Democratic turnout.[19] Moss would ultimately be defeated by a young politician named Orrin Hatch during that same election cycle and Marriott easily coasted to victory against Howe.[20] The inevitable loss for Howe was made that much worse.

If you fall short, immediately come clean and make amends with voters. Dragging out the situation longer than necessary will only make it worse

---

[17] One week prior to his arrest, Howe publicly stated his support for a stronger House Ethics Committee amidst multiple sex scandals, saying that these the incident "casts a bad light on congressional action as a whole."

[18] One of the more random internet conspiracy theories is that the LDS Church is responsible for the national prohibition on marijuana. The basics of the false theory is that when Mormons fled to Mexico to escape polygamy, some began to experiment with marijuana. Upon their return to Utah, they brought the plant with them only to have the church and state eventually outlaw it. From there, prohibition laws supposedly spread to the rest of the country. Even though a few national publications have been fooled by the story, none of it is true, as proven by one of my favorite Mormon historians Ardis Parshall.

[19] Howe had served as the chief of staff to Senator Moss before running for Congress.

[20] Approximately 40 percent of Utahns still voted for Howe despite the scandal and the Democratic Party officially endorsing a write-in candidate for the same seat. Imagine today 40 percent of the state voting for someone who had just been convicted of soliciting a prostitute.

for you and your family.[21] Sometimes your error will rise to the level of resignation, but many times your shortcomings fall far short of that.[22]

In politics, self-destructive behavior is unfortunately all too common. Sometimes there are warning signs, but other times friends and family are completely caught off guard by the behavior.

Own your mistakes immediately. There is no other path to redemption.

---

[21] One Utah County mayor was so stressed in his elected position that he took a drive alone to California to avoid the city's annual budget meetings. When asked to explain his absence, he claimed he had been the victim of a carjacking and kidnapping. After finally confessing to the hoax, the mayor was charged with filing a false claim with police.

[22] Minor peccadillos are referred to as "Taking a Trip to Franklin." This reference comes from the small border town of Franklin in southern Idaho frequented by Utah residents looking to bypass the state's stringent gambling laws. One store has a large sign inside that says, "Home of the Utah Lottery."

THE FRED MEYER RULE

Don't be dumb. And don't get the photos developed.

In the storied Holy War between the University of Utah and BYU, there has been a considerable number of pranks between the two schools. Most are good-natured, but occasionally they drift into the territory of criminal behavior.

In 2004, a red "U" was painted on "Y" mountain in Provo. The cost to repair the vandalism was an estimated $6,000. In the end, eight University of Utah baseball players were charged with felonies for defacing the mountain. The mystery was solved when one of the players dropped off camera film to be developed at a local Fred Meyer store, with photos of all of the players participating in the crime.[23]

Good-natured fun is always appreciated in Utah politics, but occasionally a political rivalry can drift into inappropriate terrain. You may be short on sleep and feeling stressed, but never resort to behavior you'll be embarrassed about in the morning.

---

[23] Also known nationally as the Stringer Bell Rule.

A SHANDON ANDERSON MOMENT

An excellent career can be overshadowed by one critical mistake.

For Utah Jazz fans, the name Shandon Anderson brings back a singular memory, a missed layup at the most crucial of times in the 1997 NBA Finals.[24] With the score tied and 28 seconds left in the pivotal Game 6, Anderson missed an easy layup. The Bulls scored on their next possession, ending the game and Utah's championship hopes.

While Anderson scored plenty of points for the Jazz during his tenure with the team, one crucial miss will always be remembered by fans.

In politics, one high-profile mistake can overshadow a career of dutiful public service. When we hear the name, Allan Howe, we don't remember any of the good legislation the former Congressman may have sponsored or the votes he took, instead we remember his police arrest which ultimately ended his political career. Avoid having a Shandon Anderson Moment by remaining focused to the very end of your time in office.

---

[24] Utahns will also remember the $50,000 fine Chicago Bulls star Dennis Rodman received from the league in the series for saying, "It's difficult to get in sync because of all the (expletive) Mormons out here. And you can quote me on that." Bulls Coach Phil Jackson made it worse by defending Rodman saying, "To Dennis, a Mormon may just be a nickname for people from Utah. He may not even know it's a religious cult or sect or whatever it is."*
*This message is approved by Mike Huckabee.

THE MANSION BATHTUB RULE

Always confront a problem head on.

As the Vietnam War raged on across the nation, colleges and universities became the epicenter of protests. Utah universities were not immune with student protests and walkouts all across the state. Daily protests occurred across Utah's campuses, and at the University of Utah one temporary building was even set on fire. On October 15, 1969, thousands of students took part in a protest and march downtown that was called at the time "the largest peace demonstration in Utah history."[25]

At around this same time, Utah Governor Cal Rampton returned from a trade mission to Japan. After a long flight, he decided to take a bath in the Governor's Mansion before turning in for the night. A knock at the bathroom door came from his wife Lucybeth who reported that a group of University of Utah students had come to the mansion to protest the war, and she had invited them inside. Governor Rampton quickly dressed and went downstairs to find 40 students sitting in the living room, some on couches and many of the rest on the floor drinking soda that the First Lady had given them.[26]

Rather than protesting the governor as they had initially planned, they sat down together and discussed the conflict in the friendly environment of the governor's living room.

Always confront a problem head on, no matter how uncomfortable you may feel. Never hide behind others in a moment of such difficulty. After all, public service was never for the faint of heart.

---

[25] Brandon Johnson, "Protesting the Vietnam War in Salt Lake," Utah Stories from the Beehive Archive. www.utahhumanities.org/stories/items/show/184.

[26] No word on whether the First Lady was Team Sodalicious or Team Swig.

CHAPTER 6

MEET THE MORMONS:
THE CHURCH OF JESUS CHRIST
OF LATTER-DAY SAINTS

THE RELEASE TIME RULE

Don't underestimate the importance of the state's predominant religion.

Across the entire state of Utah, high schools dot the arid landscape. It comes with the territory in a state that is the youngest in the country, with significantly higher birthrates than the national average. But almost without fail, next to the school is a nondescript building owned by the Church of Jesus Christ of Latter-day Saints. The buildings house the high school students' daily study of church scripture under a unique arrangement called release time.

Release time is essentially treated like any other elective course, except no high school credit is awarded. In fact, with Utah's growing student population, the release time arrangement has helped many local schools avoid the need to expand a school's physical size.

With more than 60 percent of the state's population belonging to the faith (the highest percent for any religion in the country), it is perhaps unsurprising that religion would be such an integral part of the state's culture. While religion is seldom discussed in politics, and it is taboo in the state to invoke one's faith to run for higher office, the undercurrent of personal religious belief is strong and should not be ignored.

THE MORMON MAFIA

Utahns can be relentlessly nice in their interactions with you.

During the run-up to the 2016 presidential election, *Fox News*[1] commentator Lou Dobbs expressed his frustration with independent candidate Evan McMullin's last-minute bid to win Utah's six electoral votes. Dobbs took to Twitter to say the following, "Look Deeper, He's nothing but a Globalist, Romney and Mormon Mafia Tool #MAGA #AmericaFirst #TrumpPence16 #TrumpTrain #Dobbs."[2]

Some of my favorite responses to the infamous "Mormon Mafia" line included the following:

- "They don't call them funeral potatoes for nothing...."
- "'I know you drank the coffee, Fredo. You broke my heart. You broke my heart.'"[3]
- "Just try to tell a member of the #MormonMafia that you're not interested in family board game night. See what happens."

The fact that Dobbs was immediately ridiculed across the media demonstrates how the "nice Mormon" image is widely accepted in the public mind. This image helps inform politics in the state. Direct confrontation is viewed unfavorably. Negative attacks often backfire. And never forget that niceness trumps all.[4]

---

[1] Fellow *Fox News* host Sean Hannity visited the state in 2014 in response to the controversial appearance by liberal filmmaker Michael Moore at Utah Valley University. When student leaders invited the liberal Moore to campus for his $40,000 speaking fee, university boosters and lawmakers were outraged. The visit by Hannity helped assuage those concerns, with gubernatorial hopeful Jon Huntsman Jr. picking up Hannity's $50,000 travel tab.

[2] In general, if someone feels the need to write out their own last name in a hashtag you probably shouldn't take them seriously.

[3] Another tweet from Utah Lieutenant Governor Spencer Cox said, "Highly underrated part of #MormonMafia is that most of us don't get the [R-rated] Godfather references..."

[4] There does seem to be some nuance on this point. Utahns like to send fighters to Congress, but value collaboration much more in local and statewide races.

THE PROPER ROLE OF GOVERNMENT THEORY

Dog whistles work in Utah politics.

A political dog whistle can be defined as language that is intended for one specific audience, while others are unaware of the underlying message. Politicians will frequently do this in political races to convey support to one constituency without turning off another.

The name of this theory comes from a phrase used by prominent LDS leader and Secretary of Agriculture Ezra Taft Benson. Over the years this phrase, "proper role of government," has been used by Utah politicians, first as a direct dog whistle to the John Bircher wing[5] of the Republican Party and later to those associated with the Tea Party.

A current member of Utah's congressional delegation initially campaigned with a somewhat similar tactic. While referencing the Founding Fathers, he said they were "wise men raised up unto this very purpose." The phrase didn't strike listeners as out of place, but to the Latter-day Saint ear the candidate was clearly quoting scripture.[6]

In certain instances, politics can be viewed as a zero-sum game. Are you a Tea Party Republican or an establishment Republican? Are you a Matheson Democrat or Feeling the Bern? Political races are scattered with an assortment of litmus tests that unsuspecting candidates sometimes fail to realize even exist.

---

[5] Utah Governor J. Bracken Lee once criticized the organization as follows: "I do not believe that you can fight a dictatorship – and that's all Communism is – by setting up another dictatorship. Now the whole theory behind the John Birch Society as I understand it is the only way to whip Communism is adopt their tactics."* Lee was never one to mince words about any political foe.

[6] Had the candidate indicated that he was quoting the book of scripture known as Doctrine and Covenants, many in the audience would have been turned off (including members of the LDS faith).

* Dennis L. Lythgoe, *Let 'Em Holler: A Political Biography of J. Bracken Lee* (Salt Lake City, UT: Utah State Historical Society, 1982) 245.

For the most calculating of politicians, they may try and straddle two lines through the use of dog whistles. Flirting with both sides like this can be a delicate balance, and it is best to be avoided. But don't be surprised to hear your opponent occasionally drop a well-placed dog whistle.

THE TITHE COROLLARY

Some dog whistles are less subtle than others.

To help support his environmental arguments in the 1992 U.S. Senate race, Democrat Wayne Owens made a direct appeal to religion in a campaign mailer regarding wilderness protections. In defense of environmental legislation, Owens pointed out that many Utahns supported wilderness, the sticking point was how much land was designated.

A Bureau of Land Management study recommended the designation of 1.9 million acres as wilderness, while environmentalists wanted a much larger figure. Owens pushed a bill that would designate five million acres of the state to wilderness. In response to outraged Utahns, Owens briefly turned to church practice to defend his position. He said, "About ten percent of Utah's land would be preserved as wilderness if [my bill] is passed, a tithe to our future and to our children who will never have to wonder what sort of grandeur we once lived with in Utah."[7] This did not impress church members in the Utah backcountry where Owens was soundly defeated.

Reference to religion in Utah comes with risk. When Bennett had two high-profile Democrats publicly endorse his candidacy over Owens, a draft copy of the newspaper advertisement mentioned their religious affiliation. A letter from one of the two asked that Bennett delete the church references. His reasoning: "My experience is that explicit reference to LDS service in political campaigns can backfire."

It is always best to keep a bright line between your private religious beliefs and your public policy positions.

---

[7] "Utah Outdoors," Wayne Owens Newsletter, 6 September 1989, Utah Republican State Central Committee –State Files, Officeholders – Congressman Wayne Owens, J. Willard Marriott Library.

THE DEAR BROTHER PRINCIPLE

Appealing to religion will backfire.

In the 1948 Utah gubernatorial election, former Price Mayor J. Bracken Lee decided to challenge incumbent Governor Herbert Maw. To combat the momentum from his opponent late in the race, Maw turned to religious grounds in a mailer he sent directly to voters not as governor, but "as an active and devoted member of our Church." After attacking Lee's position on alcohol regulation, Maw signed the letter, "Sincerely Your Brother."

After being called out for the letter by the Lee campaign, Maw defended it by saying he intended to send it to members of all faiths in the state. An outcry ensued over the letter and Maw ultimately failed in his bid for a third term.[8]

When used overtly, religious references can often turn voters away from a particular candidate (including many members of the same faith). Aspiring candidates should never lean on religion in order to prop up their election hopes. If you ignore this warning, voters will punish you at the ballot box.[9]

---

[8] This was actually not the first election between the two foes, as Maw narrowly defeated Lee in the 1944 gubernatorial election. In that race, a "Morals and the Mayor" pamphlet was distributed by Maw supporters. While blasting Lee's record as mayor of Price, the pamphlet concluded, "The pioneers came here for a great spiritual purpose. They left all that they had, they buried their loved ones on the plains, they met the desert and the savages, in order to satisfy the highest demands of their souls. It would betray their great purpose to place in the office of chief executive a man who has proved in his small field that he feels it profitable and fitting for government to be intimately connected with gambling and prostitution and disregard for law of the state." Dennis L. Lythgoe, *Let 'Em Holler: A Political Biography of J. Bracken Lee* (Salt Lake City, UT: Utah State Historical Society, 1982) 25-6.

[9] In a 2018 legislative race, one candidate attacked his opponent Representative Patrice Arent (the only Jewish legislator in Utah) by using language from the Book of Mormon, "Please vote in memory of our God, our religion, and freedom, our peace, our wives and our children." Utah Governor Gary Herbert immediately defended Arent who easily defeated her Republican opponent.

THE TEMPLE MAILER COROLLARY

Utah voters are especially sensitive to the use of religious symbols in political campaigns.

The infamous Temple Mailer was sent to Republican state delegates on the eve of the 2010 GOP State Convention. On one side of the postcard was a photo of Mike Lee, candidate for U.S. Senate, placed next to the Salt Lake Temple.[10] On the other side was incumbent U.S. Senator Bob Bennett next to a photo of the U.S. Capitol Building. The only text at the bottom of the postcard read, "Which candidate really has Utah values?"

Unbeknownst to delegates at the time was that a supporter of Bennett was the author of the attack ad. Most in the convention hall that day believed that someone from the Lee campaign was responsible. The author's plan depended on the assumption that Utahns are so sensitive to religious attack ads that someone could create an ad attacking one's self in order to benefit politically.

In algebra, you learn that a double negative creates a positive. Think of the Temple Mailer Corollary as the double negative principle in action.

While difficult to state the exact impact of the mailer, one of Lee's top campaign officials believed it nearly swung the entire convention vote to

---

[10] An example of out-of-state consultants struggling to understand Utah culture can be found in the excellent book, *Mia Love: The Rise, Stumble and Resurgence of the Next GOP Star* written by *Salt Lake Tribune* writers Robert Gehrke, Thomas Burr and Matt Canham. They relate the story of a potentially controversial ad that was ultimately ditched by the campaign. "One ad pitched by the out-of-state consultants featured several shots of Mia running with smiling supporters falling in behind, joining her along the way, exchanging high fives with the candidate. The problem: the LDS Oquirrh Mountain Temple was clearly visible in several scenes....The ham-handed imagery of the temple in a political ad would backfire, local campaign staff feared, and create a commotion over whether Mia was exploiting her faith" (p. 100).

Lee's opponent.[11] Lee himself called the mailer, "thuggish, Chicago-style tactics" and demanded an investigation by the Federal Election Commission.

Out-of-state consultants seldom understand how sensitive Utahns are to these attacks. As politics grows more uncivil, Utah voters provide an anomaly to the national status quo. Remember the Temple Mailer Corollary if ever tempted to attack an opponent unfairly, especially if religion is involved. Without a doubt, it will do more harm than good.

---

[11] Tim Bridgewater nearly won the convention with slightly less than the 60 percent needed to avoid a primary election.

THE CHRISTMAS CARD COROLLARY

On rare occasions, you can directly reference your religious faith.

Utahns don't expect you to run from your religion. In fact, any attempts to do so are punished. However, they are very sensitive about any perception that religion is being used to gain a political advantage.

An annual Christmas card is a unique time where politicians can be more open with their religiosity. I received several different Christmas cards last year from Utah politicians with the following examples:

- A wedding photo of a member of Congress's child with the image of an exterior wall of the Salt Lake Temple on the side of the image.
- A collage of multiple images with a small image including a member of Congress and their spouse in front of the LDS Conference Center.
- A family photo with a missionary son included in white shirt and tie.

It is critical that even in such a moment, important religious symbols are not the focal point, or you run the risk of incurring the Temple Mailer Corollary. But occasionally it is appropriate to be open with your religion. It is unquestionably a part of who you are as an individual, so long as recipients believe you are doing so sincerely and not to receive some sort of political benefit.[12]

---

[12] Never mention church callings, no matter how important they may have been. It almost always turns off voters, including Latter-day Saints. One prominent statewide official once touted his "difficult church leadership responsibilities that required many more hours a week." Everyone knows what you mean. It's bad form.

THE BARBARA SMITH ENDORSEMENT

Current Latter-day Saint leaders might not be able to endorse you, but that doesn't stop former ones from doing so.

In his 2000 reelection effort, U.S. Senator Orrin Hatch faced an angry convention crowd. To help combat the anger, he asked former president of the LDS Church's Relief Society, Barbara Smith, to deliver his nominating speech.

The crowd of angry delegates booed both Hatch and Smith, an episode that alarmed many Utahns. The experience did help Hatch explain his convention struggles to the general public, who ultimately sympathized with the candidate.[13]

A similar tactic was employed during the 2016 presidential campaign. Utah voters, especially women, struggled to support Republican Donald Trump.[14] Again, a former president of the LDS Church's Relief Society Julie Beck was asked to help. With Hatch serving as one of Trump's biggest supporters in the state, it is unsurprising that he would adopt a similar tactic as his 2000 convention speech. Beck was accompanied by former General Authority Robert Oaks, who was named an honorary chairman of the 2016 Trump campaign in Utah.[15]

While this practice has been infrequent in statewide races, it is much more common in a local election. The support of a local LDS leader can often carry considerable weight in a community where they are well respected.

---

[13] Occasionally it can make sense to step into a punch. Sometimes embracing controversy can be politically advantageous, otherwise known as the Feigned Madness of Hamlet (and Mike Noel).

[14] This characterization of events is disputed by Trump publicist John Barron.

[15] As church members struggled to justify voting for Trump, the Beck/Oaks endorsements certainly helped. In a subsequent election, Oaks endorsed Utah Representative Mike Kennedy for U.S. Senate in his bid to defeat Mitt Romney. The former Massachusetts governor easily defeated Kennedy despite the Oaks endorsement.

Of course, there is still danger in this method. In a recent Utah House of Representatives race, the Democratic candidate had yard signs with his name saying: "School Principal. Ecclesiastical Leader. Baseball Coach. Father." The words "ecclesiastical leader" was a reference to his time as a local LDS leader (stake president). The tactic was widely viewed as too heavy handed, and the candidate was defeated.

There was a time when current leaders of the church were much more active in partisan politics. Former Utah Governor J. Bracken Lee was able to garner such support, even as someone who was not a member of the faith. Apostle Ezra Taft Benson endorsed Lee in his challenge against the incumbent Herbert Maw in the 1940s saying, "Generally, the Church prefers a non-Mormon with high principles to a Jack Mormon."[16] Another apostle and member of the faith's First Presidency, Hugh B. Brown, frequently campaigned in support of Democratic candidates including his delivery of the keynote address at the 1958 state Democratic convention.

Partisan political involvement of current church leaders eventually ceased with leaders only rarely engaging on specific political issues, not candidates. Today, even local leaders are very cautious about their support of political candidates.

---

[16] Dennis L. Lythgoe, *Let 'Em Holler: A Political Biography of J. Bracken Lee* (Salt Lake City, UT: Utah State Historical Society, 1982) 24.

THE TWIN RELICS OF BARBARISM RULE

Latter-day Saints are overwhelmingly Republican.[17]

When the Republican Party was first organized in 1856, its initial platform called for getting rid of the "twin relics of barbarism, polygamy and slavery."[18]

Several decades later in 1884, the Republican Party again blasted Utahns saying, "It is the duty of Congress to enact such laws as shall promptly and effectually suppress the system of polygamy within our Territories; and divorce the political from the ecclesiastical power of the so-called Mormon Church, and that the law so enacted should be rigidly enforced by the civil authorities if possible, and by the military if need be."[19] Four years later, the party said, "The political power of the Mormon Church in the Territories as exercised in the past is a menace to free institutions too dangerous to be longer suffered."[20] These two pronouncements represent the first and only times in American history that a major party platform has condemned a specific religion.

The irony is not lost on many Utahns that the Republican Party was founded with the intention of ridding the nation of Mormons, and yet members of the faith are overwhelmingly members of the same party today.

---

[17] This has not always been the case in Utah's history. In one memorable election (1936), Utah elected 78 Democrats to the Legislature and only five Republicans. If you think it's lonely being a Democrat today in the Legislature, imagine what caucus meeting felt like for William H. Griffin, the only Republican in the entire 1938 Utah State Senate.

[18] Technically, the platform called for the elimination of these two evils in territories, not necessarily the nation as a whole, but it clearly intended to set the country on that path.

[19] George E. Condon Jr., "Republicans Weren't Always Accepting of Mormons." *The Atlantic*, 27 August 2012.

[20] Ibid.

THE PROHIBITION RULE

Utah voters occasionally disagree with the state's major religion.

Liquor laws have a storied history in the Beehive State from Zion Curtains to private clubs and everything in between.[21] With a majority of Utahns belonging to a church that shuns alcohol consumption, it perhaps comes as no surprise that alcohol policy would be quite conservative.

But in a somewhat ironic twist, Utahns also cast the deciding vote to repeal Prohibition in 1933.[22] A constitutional amendment needs three-fourths of states to ratify its passage, and Utah was the final state to push the country over this threshold.

This came despite the opposition of LDS Church President Heber J. Grant.[23] Leading up to the 1933 public vote, several speeches during the faith's general conference focused on a commandment to avoid alcohol and the need for members to continue support of Prohibition.

In the end, the vote total wasn't even close. In a state with 66 percent of its residents belonging to the LDS faith, 62 percent of residents voted to repeal Prohibition, much to the disappointment of President Grant.[24] While the LDS Church undoubtedly has tremendous influence in Utah, there are times when residents go against their leader's wishes. This occurs infrequently, in part because the church becomes involved in politics in only very rare circumstances.[25]

---

[21] This is a book, not a bar.

[22] The headline from an international newspaper at the time said, "'Prohibition Is Dead! Mormons Killed It! Whoopee! Happy Days Are Here Again!'"

[23] Grant was the father-in-law to U.S. Senator Wallace Bennett and grandfather of U.S. Senator Bob Bennett.

[24] Grant became used to political disappointment as he openly campaigned against President Franklin D. Roosevelt multiple times. Despite his opposition, Utah voted for the Democrat in each of his victorious elections. Grant called the experience, "One of the most serious conditions that has confronted me since I became President of the Church."

[25] Their lobbyists in Utah's Capitol have been jokingly known as the "Home Teachers."

THE MX MISSILE RULE

The Church of Jesus Christ of Latter-day Saints occasionally engages in unexpected issues.

In 1979, the U.S. Air Force announced its plans to build a new intercontinental ballistic missile system in rural Utah. The massive, multibillion-dollar nuclear weapons project would dramatically change Beaver and Millard Counties along with numerous surrounding communities.

At first, the project received support from many of Utah's political leaders with tremendous economic benefits at stake.[26] But opposition began to emerge, in particular among the communities nearest the proposal as Utah would become a potential major target in any future attack from the Soviet Union.

The death knell to the project came several years later when the Church of Jesus Christ of Latter-day Saints announced their opposition to the project. The church's 1981 statement said the following, "Our fathers came to this western area to establish a base from which to carry the gospel of peace to the peoples of the earth. It is ironic, and a denial of the very essence of that gospel, that in this same general area there should be constructed a mammoth weapons system potentially capable of destroying much of civilization."

While the prevailing view of Utah from outside the state is that the church controls every facet of state government, the truth is the faith rarely engages on issues of importance in the state. When they do, the issue is almost always associated with a moral concern.

---

[26] One member of Utah's congressional delegation said at the time of those opposing the project, "[They are] people with their heads in the sand." Another member of the delegation said, "Reasonable people would have to conclude we've got to have the MX." It was Utah's lone female State Senator, Frances Farley, who first opposed the measure.

PULLING A HUCKABEE

Utahns are especially sensitive to any perceived attack on religion.

Former presidential candidate Mike Huckabee is perhaps one of Utah's most vilified candidates in recent memory, due to his subtle anti-Mormon rhetoric during the 2008 presidential race against Mitt Romney.

When asked about Romney's faith, Huckabee replied, "I really don't know much about it." He then asked the reporter, "Don't Mormons believe that Jesus and the devil are brothers?"

While claiming it was an innocent question, the former Baptist minister knew exactly what he was doing in a classic dog whistle to evangelicals across the country. Soon after the Huckabee comments, a BYU poll revealed that Utah voters preferred Democratic candidate Barack Obama over the Republican Huckabee, 58-42 percent.

Utah's history with anti-Mormon bigotry has the state's population on high alert for any smear against its largest religion. Some might characterize it as a persecution complex, but when people like Mike Huckabee take advantage of lingering anti-Mormon sentiments you can understand their sensitivity.[27]

---

[27] Pro tip: never hold a political rally near Temple Square unless you want to lose the state's LDS vote. There's a reason leaders of the church prefer hosting prominent political leaders at Welfare Square. The symbol of the temple next to any political message will be immediately rejected by members of the faith.

THE JFK TABERNACLE COROLLARY

Showing even a slight understanding of the state's history goes a long way with Utahns.

Several months before the 1960 presidential election, John F. Kennedy traveled to Salt Lake City, where he delivered an address at the city's prominent Tabernacle on Temple Square, the home of the Church of Jesus Christ of Latter-day Saint's general conferences.

In a memorable speech, Kennedy referenced many of the faith's key tenets and past encounters with political persecution. Kennedy began with the story of Reed Smoot, a former U.S. Senator and apostle of the church, who was forced to endure a three-year U.S. Senate investigation of his faith.[28] Kennedy said:

"I am thinking of Apostle Reed Smoot – and those who challenged his right to a seat in the U.S. Senate, charging that he would subordinate the claims of his country to the claims of his church. They did not know – or would not hear – that the 101st section of the Latter Day Saints Doctrine and Covenants gave a scriptural preeminence to the Constitution and its oaths. But fortunately the forces of reason and tolerance enabled him to take his seat. And in the years that followed, Senator Smoot earned the respect and affection of every Senator who had challenged him. He rose to be dean of the Senate and chairman of its powerful Committee on Finance – and no voice was ever heard to say that he had not been devoted solely to the public good as he saw it. The story of Reed Smoot symbolizes the long struggle of the Mormon people for religious liberty. They suffered persecution and exile, at the hands of Americans whose own ancestors, ironically enough, had fled here to escape the curse of intolerance. But they never faltered in their devotion to the principle of

---

[28] While the U.S. Senate committee recommended that Smoot be removed from office on religious grounds, the full Senate voted to keep him in office in a 43-27 vote. The lengthy hearings included a public interrogation of the church's President Joseph F. Smith.

religious liberty – not for themselves alone, but for all mankind. And in the 11ᵗʰ Article of Faith, Prophet Joseph Smith not only declared in ringing tones: 'We claim the privilege of worshipping Almighty God according to the dictates of our own conscience' – he also set forth the belief that all men should be allowed 'the same privilege. Let them worship how, where, or what they may.'"

Kennedy's recognition of church history and doctrine was appreciated by members of the faith across the state. While he didn't win the state in November, he received 45 percent of Utah's vote.[29]

Taking the time to understand the state's history is an easy way to impress Utahns. You don't need to know everything, but just showing that you cared enough to understand something small means a lot to Utah residents.

---

[29] Eight years later, the former president's brother Robert F. Kennedy would visit Brigham Young University during his own presidential campaign. He was treated like a rock star with 15,000 people packed into the George Albert Fieldhouse to hear his speech. In a reference to the political opposition he received from President Lyndon B. Johnson, Kennedy jokingly compared himself to Brigham Young, "And now I too know how it is to take on Johnson's army," a reference to the arrival of Johnston's Army in the 1857 Utah War. He concluded his speech with this memorable line, "It was once said of Utah (of the hard soil and the tribulation of your pioneers) that life does not come easy. Perhaps some of the special flavor of Utah comes from this quality that things come hard."

THE CAFÉ RIO REMINDER

Utahns have a proud tradition of public service.

If you're ever feeling lonely as a young campaign staffer in Washington D.C. far away from your Utah home, go visit one of the eight recently opened Café Rios in the D.C. metropolitan area. The Utah-based company has numerous locations throughout the West, but only has one other restaurant east of the Rockies,[30] besides the D.C. locations.

Why the significant number of restaurants in this one location, when so many other eastern cities have none? The answer is simple. A sizeable number of transplanted Utahns now live in Washington D.C., with one part of nearby Virginia affectionately known as "Little Provo."

I recently went to one of these D.C. Café Rios and was not surprised to see several patrons of the restaurant wearing shirts and sweatshirts from various Utah schools (but mostly BYU, let's be honest). Prominent journalist McKay Coppins once jokingly estimated that nearly 50 percent of the restaurant's patrons at any hour of the day were members of the Church of Jesus Christ of Latter-day Saints, likely with ties back to Utah.

The church connection potentially helps explain the high number of Utahns working in Washington D.C. With a high language proficiency thanks to church missions, Washington D.C. is home to many international organizations where foreign ties and language skills are a must. And while the church shies away from formal positions on most political issues, members are encouraged to be involved in public service.

So as a Utahn, if you're ever feeling alone while out in our nation's capital, take a short drive over to Café Rio and you'll feel right at home.

---

[30] The other location is Orlando, Florida near Disney World, a frequent stop for Utahns.*
*An entire song in *The Book of Mormon* Broadway musical is dedicated to the city of Orlando.

THE HINCKLEY RULE

Even Latter-day Saints believe there needs to be a separation of church and state.

Soon after his election as governor of the state of Utah, Mike Leavitt was invited to meet with Gordon B. Hinckley, leader of the Church of Jesus Christ of Latter-day Saints. During the conversation, Leavitt related the advice given to him by President Hinckley, "Governor, I have a suggestion on how we conduct business. You run the state, and we'll run the church."

While Utah's culture is dramatically impacted by the state's largest church, Utahns by and large believe that the church should rarely engage in the political process.

Utahns who don't belong to the state's largest faith are understandably sensitive to the interaction of elected officials and leaders of the church. For example, recent polling on a statewide medical marijuana initiative showed that when the church came out in opposition to the measure, support for the initiative significantly increased among those who do not belong to the faith.

While the church remains politically powerful in the state, its full weight is more often felt in its cultural importance rather than official edicts from church headquarters.

CHAPTER 7

CONSULTANTS

THE UTAHAN ERROR

It's easy to spot an out-of-state campaign consultant.

One of the easiest ways to see if a campaign is being run by someone from out of state is a simple spelling error. Traditional spell checks indicate that the extra "a" is needed in the word "Utahn," but natives know otherwise. It's a simple measure, but it has a bigger impact in many other ways.

Campaign consultants can be invaluable to a fledgling campaign. They can get things done, quickly and efficiently. Those campaign mailers, television commercials, radio ads and so many other things take a significant amount of work to execute. If a candidate has never done any of those things, the process can be daunting. The speed at which a campaign comes doesn't allow much time for delays.

However, with that same efficiency often comes a cookie-cutter approach to politics that isn't that effective in Utah. I remember watching the television commercials of a recent congressional race in Utah and recognized identical video footage in an Idaho campaign from the same election cycle. The consultant simply recycled the same video clip all across the country. No Utah red rock. No majestic Wasatch mountains.

Consultants can be extremely valuable to any campaign but look out for the Utahan Error. Without a local touch, you will miss out on important opportunities to connect with Utah voters.

THE DAVE HANSEN RULE

First-time candidates can be led astray by consultants looking to make an easy buck.

Any well-funded candidate for a congressional or statewide race will immediately be courted by various campaign consultants who are anxious to sell their services. More often than not, you will usually find the likeable Dave Hansen standing right beside the new candidate.

In fairness to Hansen, he is a brilliant tactician on the politics of a state Republican convention,[1] while that success has been less noticeable in subsequent primary[2] or general[3] elections. He is also a steady hand who has the respect of national Republican groups.

Hansen has as good a nose for money as anyone in the business, and you'll need money if you want to win. But frequently a consultant's business plan is to find a well-funded person and flatter them into running.[4] Each time the candidate is easily defeated, and yet the consultant emerges with a significant paycheck.

These consultants can be enormously valuable, especially as the candidate looks to immediately scale an operation with little to no experience in simple tasks, such as large-scale mailing, phone banks, TV and radio advertisements. Without them, your mailings will be late and your ad buy may never materialize.

---

[1] The 2012 Republican convention by U.S. Senator Orrin Hatch was unquestionably a political masterpiece.

[2] After defeating the incumbent governor in the 2016 state GOP convention, his candidate's campaign would go on to lose the primary election by a 44-percent margin.

[3] In 2014, his candidate started with significantly higher name identification and raised more than six times as much money in one of the most Republican districts in the country, only to win the race by a narrow five-percent margin.

[4] Prominent political scientist Adam Sheingate's book *Building a Business of Politics* shares the advice from one consultant, "There's nothing better than a scared, rich candidate."

Be especially cautious of the consultant who stands to financially benefit from excessive spending. In such cases, the candidate will often be advised to spend more and more, leading to an even bigger commission for the consultant.

If you have enough money, consultants will always devise new ways to spend it. Even if you set a budget at the beginning of the race, don't be surprised to find them pushing the issue as your back is against the wall late in the contest. It takes a strong candidate to keep such mercenaries in check.

THE PINK FLOYD RULE

Be yourself. Utahns value authenticity.

The Pink Floyd Rule doesn't derive its name from the rock music legend, but instead a pink flamingo who escaped from the Tracy Aviary in 1990 and lived out the remainder of his days on the Great Salt Lake. The bird, named Pink Floyd, avoided numerous attempts to return him to captivity.

While the Chilean flamingo would leave the state during summer months, he returned to the shores of the Great Salt Lake each winter for more than a decade. Some creative Utahns, calling themselves the Friends of Floyd, raised $50,000 to bring 25 additional flamingoes from Chile to join their pink friend. Running into bureaucratic hurdles, the group's efforts never came to fruition.[5]

Pink Floyd's escape from captivity and lonely existence serves as a good metaphor for the need to be yourself, no matter lonely you may feel.

A prominent psychology experiment showed that when a person enters an elevator with several people facing the rear of an elevator, the stranger will frequently turn around and model the same behavior. Unfortunately, many political campaigns are still facing the back of the elevator. Some will encourage you to be just like their most memorable winning campaign, no matter how different the current political climate may be.

It turns out, people appreciate authenticity. Be yourself, and voters will reward you.

---

[5] Apparently introducing non-native species to an environment is a bad idea. Just ask Utah Lake.

THE FUNERAL POTATO RULE

Some things look like they would never work together, but trust us, Utahns know what we're doing.

Once a week, U.S. Senators from each political party gather together for their weekly caucus lunch. They discuss policy and strategy on the issues of the day. One U.S. Senator gets to host the weekly event, with food provided from their home state.

When it's Utah's turn, staples always include Utah beef, Aggie Ice Cream and if they want to go for the full cliché, green Jell-O.

When I worked for then-U.S. Senator Bob Bennett, we of course decided to serve funeral potatoes. Later that afternoon, the front desk office phone rang and the staffer recognized the number as coming from Senate Majority Leader Bill Frist's office. Quickly picking up the phone, the staffer for the majority leader got to the point, "Senator Frist wants to know if you all have a recipe for those potatoes."

The legend only continues to grow. The food has reached such iconic status that a special 2002 Olympics pin was dedicated to the unique dish.[6]

Some out-of-state consultants read about the need to be nice in Utah, and they assume that it is just the naive at work. They tell you that you need to attack more. They want you to ditch the squeaky-clean exterior. The power struggle that occurs in virtually every competitive congressional or statewide election inevitably has this same debate. When that time comes, just remember sour cream and corn flakes. I know it shouldn't work. But just ask Bill Frist. Utahns know exactly what they're doing.

---

[6] Unfortunately, I'm convinced the name funeral potatoes has an inherent public relations problem. The name is derived from its frequent serving at after-funeral dinners prepared by a local Latter-day Saint congregation's Relief Society.

THE CROWN BURGER COROLLARY

Contrary to popular belief, Utah is not a monolithic community.

Many outsiders come to Utah thinking we're all Mormons eating our green Jell-O with shaved carrots.[7] But truth be told, the state has much more to its culture than meets the eye. In a 2009 *New York Times* article on Utah's food scene, the writer ignored the usual references of food culture (sorry fry sauce) and instead focused on an under-recognized staple of Utah's gastronomic culture – the pastrami burger.

While its origin story remains somewhat in question, Utah is unquestionably home to the widest acceptance of the culinary creation. You cannot make it more than a few blocks in Salt Lake City without passing one of the many chains of Greek hamburger restaurants in the state: Crown Burger, Apollo Burger, Astro Burger, Olympus Burger, and far too many other options to list here.[8]

Utah's Greek community has a proud tradition, including the state's annual Greek Fest held in downtown Salt Lake City. Traveling to the state during the turn of the century, many Greeks came to work in Utah mines. In the 1910 census, Utah, Wyoming and Nevada had the highest percentage of Greeks per capita in the nation.[9] While the Latter-day Saint narrative may seem overwhelming at times, there are numerous undercurrents in the state's political system.[10]

---

[7] Can we all admit that pretty much no one under 50 in the state eats Jell-O anymore?

[8] The *New York Times* piece mentioned, "Greek influence is so strong in the local restaurant industry that Mandarin, a Chinese restaurant, serves baklava."

[9] One of Utah's most successful entrepreneurs is Fred Lampropoulos. However, before he became the enormously successful CEO we all know today, his parents struggled to get by and received much-needed help from the local Greek community. Now, he is one of Utah's best-known benefactors and a former candidate for governor.

[10] One of my favorite one-liners comes from Utah's first Jewish Governor Simon Bamberger. During his 1916 campaign, he was criticized by a local mayor (and Mormon) for being a "damned Gentile." Bamberger quickly responded, "As a Jew, I have been called many a bad name, but this is the first time in my life I have been called a damned Gentile."

THE DOUBLE Z THEORY

Utahns have a habit of overdoing a trend, before eventually course correcting.

The Double Z Theory derives its name from the significant number of Utah sports teams and other organizations that decided to use the letters "zz" in their names. Before they were the "Bees," we all remember the Salt Lake Buzz. But who can forget the Utah Starzz (WNBA), the Utah Freezz (soccer), Utah Blitzz (soccer), St. George Pioneerzz[11] (baseball), Utah Catzz (indoor football), Utah Grizzlies (hockey) and of course the Utah Jazz.[12]

For a while it all seemed so clever, but then it got to be a little too cute and eventually mildly annoying. Wisely, the state has moved on and when selecting team names it's quite rare for a team to pursue the Double Z.[13]

In Utah politics, we can be slow to realize a trend has been overdone. I'm sure those baseball jersey campaign shirts were cool at one time. Cowboy hats for delegates were creative that first convention. But from time to time, you need to zig when everyone else is zagging.

We often run a campaign that is almost identical to the last one in the state or town that was victorious. This inevitably leads to redundancy and a slow transition to newer, more effective tactics.

---

[11] When Pioneerzz came out, I think this is when the state officially jumped the shark(zz).
[12] For some unknown reason, a few other sports teams have gone for a single z instead of the traditional zz (Utah Blitz - women's football, Orem Owlz - minor league baseball, Utah Blaze - arena football). The Orem Owlz even went so far as to name their team mascot, "Hootz." Please make it stop.
[13] Similarly, think of all of those Mormon-themed movies that came out in the early 2000s. What started as a trickle of fun new movies quickly became a flood of boring retreads. People stopped watching them long before the movies stopped coming (I'm looking at you, *Sons of Provo*).*
* My brother may have had a brief cameo in this not-so-hit film. Watch the first few minutes for a guy holding a baby (my nephew Brady), while singing the song "Amazing Grace."

THE HARTLEY RULE

It is difficult to keep a secret in Utah politics.

Transparency is indisputably critical in government, as sunlight provides one of the most effective disinfectants against corruption. But occasionally – especially as strategy is still being developed – it is imperative that confidences can be kept.

There is a direct correlation between the number of people who know a secret and the likelihood the secret will be divulged. The larger the group, the greater the plausible deniability and possibility that bread crumbs will be traced back to you.

Unless of course the person you're dealing with exercises the Hartley Rule, named for Utah House Chief of Staff Greg Hartley.

Politicos often want to befriend members of the media. The more information they share, the more likely they are to receive favorable coverage, or so they believe. During a contentious battle over the issue of Medicaid expansion in 2015, the Utah House Republican caucus dealt with leak after leak on the issue. So House Chief of Staff Greg Hartley had an idea. Rather than share the same information with everyone, he would divulge slightly different details to different audiences. The goal was simple: track down who was leaking the information to the media.[14]

Information is the currency that many politicos trade in. Violate the confidence of those who share it with you at your own peril.

---

[14] This strategy was also employed in the popular TV show *Game of Thrones* by the character Tyrion in the event Hartley was looking for creative inspiration.

THE MARK HOFFMAN RULE

The art of the misdirection seldom works.

On October 15, 1985, one of world's most sophisticated forgers, Mark Hoffman, murdered two prominent Utahns in cold blood. His first victim was Steven Christensen, a local businessman and documents collector to whom Hoffman owed a collection of letters supposedly written by an apostle from the early LDS Church. The second victim was Kathleen Sheets, the wife of Christensen's business partner, Gary Sheets.

Hoffman's first murder was motivated by a desire to remove financial difficulties, but the fraudster had no relationship or other motive with the Kathleen Sheets murder other than to distract law enforcement from his true identity. The attempt at misdirection was quickly foiled when Hoffman accidentally detonated a third bomb in his car the following day, seriously injuring himself. Hoffman would be sentenced to life in prison at the Utah State Prison for committing the crimes.

The biggest mistakes a campaign makes are usually initiated by those looking to be too clever. Perhaps it's an anonymous attack ad or letter. It might be a whisper campaign intended to conceal the true identity of the source. A good rule of thumb is that the person talking about the leak is the person most likely to be leaking. Similar to the criminal who feels the need to return to the scene of the crime, you want to fix the problem that you created.[15]

Part of what makes a political consultant so valuable is their ability to sift through the signal and the noise in a campaign, what's real and what isn't. With rampant misinformation and false flags from an opposing campaign, it can be difficult to discern this important difference.

---

[15] When an anonymous source is quoted in a Utah political story, I can guess who it is nine times out of ten. If you think you're fooling people, usually you're not. As former LDS Church President Harold B. Lee said, "The hit bird flutters."

THE MAC HADDOW RULE

Don't be afraid to choose an untested campaign manager.

Some of Utah's most impressive campaigns have been run by young, inexperienced campaign managers. In 1976, a 25-year old Mike Leavitt would run his father's unsuccessful bid for governor.[16] Congressman Dan Marriott turned to Leavitt two years later to run his own race. Longtime U.S. Senator Jake Garn admired the younger Leavitt's impressive operation and asked him to lead his own reelection effort soon thereafter, a relationship that would change the entire trajectory of the future governor's life.

Around that same time, Orrin Hatch surprised everyone in the state with a come-from-behind victory in the 1976 U.S. Senate race. The person he depended on in that impressive campaign was another 25-year old, BYU student and Pittsburgh native Mac Haddow.[17]

And more recently, Jason Chaffetz beat longtime incumbent Congressman Chris Cannon, thanks in no small part to a strong base of volunteers, including a young campaign director, Deidre Henderson, and campaign manager Jennifer Scott. Henderson would lead the Chaffetz campaign to easy reelections in the years that followed.

In each case, the appointments came out of necessity. The fledgling campaigns couldn't afford the most established political consultants in the state, and so they settled for bright young leaders who would do their best to help the campaign stay afloat. Looking back, they were far more successful than their more traditional counterparts. If you want to be innovative, fresh eyes are a necessity.

---

[16] Years later, a 30-year old Leavitt organized a Republican fundraiser with Bob Wright. The 1981 dinner theme was "Utahns Making America Great Again."
[17] Haddow later served in the Utah Legislature and federal prison.

THE IN-N-OUT RULE

Trends usually arrive in Utah about five years after everywhere else.

Unpopular opinion alert. In-N-Out[18] Burger is a less than ideal dining experience. There's always a long line, the options are limited, and the food really isn't all that great.

I get it. Growing up, the occasional pilgrimage to In-N-Out in California was exciting because you returned with the fun T-shirt, and you got to tell your friends about the secret menu. But with an In-N-Out now seemingly in every Utah suburb today, the novelty of visiting the restaurant has worn off.

Trends ebb and flow, including in the field of politics. What's cool today will appear dated tomorrow. Often in Utah culture, the trends seem to arrive just a little bit later than other parts of the country.[19] Stay true to your own style and personality. Pretending to be someone else never works out, and frankly, by the time you impersonate them the political tides have likely changed course.

---

[18] Not to be confused with the In-N"-Out Burger.
[19] In elementary school, my family visited a friend of my parents in Fresno, California, where I was introduced for the first time to pogs. Five years later, pogs took off at my Utah school.

THE THOMAS SEYMOUR PRINCIPLE

Things change quickly in Utah politics. Evolve with the times or be left behind.

At the end of the 19th century, Thomas Seymour grew up in rural Summit County where his family would occasionally make the three-day trek to Salt Lake City by a team of oxen. In his twenties, he found employment delivering the mail on a horse-drawn wagon on his Summit County route between Kamas and Park City. Years later, he would continue delivering mail but with a new form of transportation, a truck.[20]

He eventually moved to Salt Lake City and towards the end of his career operated a restaurant at the new Salt Lake City Airport. A 1972 *Deseret News* article reported that Seymour was once invited on a flight where he was allowed to take the controls of the airplane for a brief period of time. "He may be...the only man who has ever flown an airplane and driven oxen," the article stated.

While some key political principles likely never change, other strategies and tactics evolve much more quickly than even experts realize. Too many campaigns are still operating with a plan built for the 1980s rather than today. Part of this political atrophy occurs due to the lack of frequent competitive elections in the state. Necessity is the key driver of innovation, and Utah's one-party dominant nature has created very little necessity (and, consequently, very little innovation).[21]

---

[20] I owe this reference to the excellent historians Charles S. Peterson and Brian Q. Cannon who provide a compelling look at Utah's history in their recent book, *The Awkward State of Utah: Coming of Age in the Nation, 1896-1945*. The story of Thomas Seymour can be found in the book's introduction.

[21] Meanwhile, the skills learned by nationwide campaign experts in the trenches of other states' competitive elections are often not transferable to Utah politics. One exception to this would be Utah Clean Air Executive Director Thom Carter, a former New Jersey elected official. His broad-based experience coupled with an astute understanding of Utah politics makes him a go-to resource for innovative campaign strategies in the state.

For example, the biggest risk to most political candidates in the last few decades has been the Republican state and county conventions where party delegates winnowed the pool of candidates and frequently selected the nominee. Many of the political instincts developed by Utah experts revolve around this biennial event. Once a candidate was the Republican nominee, the outcome of the race was often no longer in doubt.[22]

Quite a few political campaigns are still driving around their team of oxen, ignoring marketplace trends that could dramatically improve their voter outreach and other campaign efforts. If you want to succeed, remember to continue evolving with the electorate or risk being left behind.

---

[22] With one congressional race often being the exception.

EPILOGUE

While it is helpful to learn these principles and theories, you must also remember that the rules of Utah politics are always evolving. What is true today may become obsolete tomorrow. This can occur through radical changes, but typically these subtle transformations are evolutionary in nature.

The lessons outlined in this book are also in no way intended to be exhaustive. The more I read of Utah political history, the more I continue to learn. At the very least, I hope this book encourages you to continue digging in your own quest to learn more about the political history of such a peculiar state.

To those men and women in the arena fighting to make the Utah of tomorrow better than it is today, thank you. I have confidence that our state's future is incredibly bright because of your selfless service.

And finally to the next generation of Utah leaders, both young and old, I hope you find this book both accessible and encouraging. We need more of you involved in state and local government if we ever expect to solve the many problems we are sure to face. There is no better time than the present to get involved. I promise you won't regret it.

ABOUT THE AUTHOR

Jon Cox is Vice President of Government Affairs at Rocky Mountain Power. He previously served as a member of the Utah House of Representatives, Sanpete County Commission and was a staff member for both Utah Governor Gary Herbert and former U.S. Senator Bob Bennett. He is a former assistant professor of history at Snow College and instructor of Utah history at the University of Utah.

Made in the USA
Middletown, DE
13 July 2019